THE

CALL TO

CHRISTIAN

PERFECTION

The Call to Christian Perfection

ISBN-13: 978-0615846194
ISBN-10: 061584619X

Cover Design by PureLight Graphics

Apprehending Truth Publishers
PO Box 249
Brookfield, Missouri 64628

Heritage of Truth Books is an imprint of
Apprehending Truth Publishers
http://www.ApprehendingTruth.net

AT 10 9 8 7 6 5 4 3 2 1
070513

The Essential Samuel Chadwick Collection
from
Heritage of Truth™

The Way to Pentecost
The Call to Christian Perfection
The Path of Prayer
Humanity and God

This edition of
The Call to Christian Perfection by Samuel Chadwick is

A Heritage of Truth Book
Reclaiming the Wisdom of the Past

Heritage of Truth
Reclaiming the Wisdom of the Past

Apprehending Truth Publishers
Brookfield, Missouri

THE
CALL TO
CHRISTIAN
PERFECTION

Samuel Chadwick

CONTENTS

The Accent of Wesley's Teaching

Weslyanism was born of God in the warmed heart of its founder. It grew with his growth. All its developments have their correspondence in his experience. Membership is based on personal conversion, the ordinances are ordered for the nourishing of the soul, and all things are made subservient to the bringing of men to the knowledge of the truth.

John Wesley had no doctrinal eccentricities. To the end he was an orthodox clergyman of the Church of England. He protested that he had always been loyal to both her doctrine and her discipline. He made no new discovery, invented no new theory, denied no dogma. The peculiarity of his teaching lay in its accent. It gave a new emphasis. It proclaimed the old truth with a living voice, spoken out of the depths of a living soul. Academic truth kills; truth vitalized by experience quickens and saves, Wesley preached Christ as he had realized Him in his own soul. The Weslyan doctrines of conversion, assurance, and full salvation can be traced to marked crises in his own experience of the saving grace of God. The Weslyan peculiarities of fellowship, testimony, and aggression, were all first exemplified in the religious life of the first Weslyan. He is the explanation of every essential peculiarity of the great Weslyan movement. He anticipated the developments of two hundred years, and every forward movement is discovered to be but a return to first principles.

❧ The Democracy of the Kingdom ❧

The first distinctive note of his creed was the universality of the gospel of Christ. He who claimed the world for his parish preached a gospel worthy of the claim. Christ died for all; the gates of the eternal kingdom were flung wide for all; the feast of the Father's house was spread for all. There was no limitation, exemption, or preference. He had heard the voice of God commanding him to go forth everywhere, calling upon all men to turn and live. The secret of his confidence was his own experience of the grace of God. From the moment he himself was accepted, he was debtor to all, and despaired of none.

It is difficult for us to realize the startling novelty of such teaching in Wesley's day. To us it is a commonplace; to the eighteenth century it was a revelation. It was novel as a doctrine, and still more novel as a testimony. The England to which the great revival came was wrapped in dense darkness. Rationalism[1] had quenched the altar fire, and brutality had taken possession of the people. The dissenting Churches were taking their ease after their heroic struggles with principalities

---

[1] The theory that the exercise of reason, rather than experience, authority, or spiritual revelation, provides the primary basis for knowledge. (The American Heritage® Dictionary of the English Language, Fourth Edition copyright ©2000 by Houghton Mifflin Company. Updated in 2009. Published by Houghton Mifflin Company.)

and powers. In the zeal for liberty the zeal for souls had suffered loss, and in the reaction it was not regained. If the Established Church was asleep in the dark, the Dissenters were as truly asleep in the light. In both Churches there were some who were awake. Bishop Butler had answered and routed the deists, and in many a sanctuary the candle of the Lord was kept alight. But religion was a thing apart, and its followers were elect and separate from the common ruck of men. Calvinism was the dominant creed, and Calvinism in its baldest form means monopoly, privilege, caste. Wesley fought Calvinism with all his might, and better still, he preached everywhere the gospel of universal love. It brought to men a new conception of God, gave them a new idea of religion, and, not least, it revealed to them the value of manhood in the sight of God. It offered salvation to all on equal terms. It was for the boy in the stable, as much as for the heir in the palace; for the man at the plow as truly as for the man in the pulpit; for the sinner in the gutter, as well as for the saint in the curtained pew. The word startled men into life. Respectable people were shocked beyond measure, for respectability is always ready to imagine itself entitled to a monopoly of heaven's favor and gifts. Pious people were scandalized that the vulgar and reprobate should be welcomed to the privileges of the Father's house. Still, they came, and the land was filled with the hallelujahs of converted ruffians who had wept their way back to God. Wesley was the first great evangelist in this country to whom was given the privilege of preaching through the length and breadth of the land this glorious gospel in which there is no restriction, limitation, or reserve. What John preached, Charles sang. The Weslyan Hymn-book is the manual of Weslyan theology and the expression of Weslyan experience. The hymns everywhere strike the note of universality. Listen to this:

> Come, sinners, to the gospel feast,
> Let every soul be Jesus' guest;
> Ye need not one be left behind,
> For God hath bidden all mankind.
>
> Sent by my Lord, on you I call;
> The invitation is for all:
> Come, all the world; come, sinner, thou!
> All things in Christ are ready now;

There is no possibility of mistaking the invitation, and the same note runs through all their songs. They went everywhere, saying to every man:

> "O let me commend my Saviour to you."

Wesley did not give himself to academic discussion, but to the preaching of the Word, and by his persistent testimony he gave the death-blow to the doctrine which limited the possibility of salvation to the favored few.

❧ An Assured Salvation ❧

Not less conspicuous than the doctrine of universality

was Wesley's teaching of Assurance. Not only might every man be saved, but it was his privilege to be conscious of his acceptance in Christ. This was a prominent feature of Wesley's own conversion. Here is his own account of it: "In the evening I went very unwillingly to a Society in Aldersgate Street, where one was reading Luther's preface to the Epistle to the Romans. About a quarter before nine, while he was describing the change which God works in the heart, through faith in Christ, I felt my heart strangely warmed. I felt I did trust in Christ, Christ alone, for salvation; and an assurance was given me that He had taken away my sins, even mine, and saved me from the law of sin and death."[2]

An assurance was given him, and to that assurance he testified openly on the spot. He lived in the enjoyment of an assured acceptance, and preached its privilege to all who would trust in Christ, Christ alone, for salvation. This also gave great offense and occasion of stumbling, but the Weslyans exulted and sang with the gladness of those who know. Some, doubtless, dwelt in a false security, and mistook emotion for divine impression. Here and there the corresponding evidence of righteousness was wanting. In every movement which stirs the soul's depths there are those who take up professions without conviction, but multitudes rejoiced in the witness of God's Spirit to their adoption. Wesley fostered their faith, fanned their enthusiasm, and guarded at every point against fanaticism. Those who testified loudly and walked crookedly he mercilessly expelled. On the other hand, he urged all to seek

[2] John Wesley's Journal, note on Friday, May 19, 1738, A reference to the following Wednesday, May 24.

the full assurance of faith, and to make open confession of the same. The converts were gathered into Society Classes, where all spoke frankly of the experience of God in the soul. Love-feasts became great rallying centers, where men and women testified of the wonderful works of God. No wonder they sang! They were children of God and heirs of heaven. Poverty lost its sting in the vision of glory. All distinctions of rank, wealth, and culture disappeared. All were one in Christ. The Weslyan people became a brotherhood; a radiant jubilant family of God. The witness of the Spirit is now conceded to be the privilege of sonship by all the evangelical churches, but it was the Wesleys who brought it to the people. Wherever Weslyans gathered, it was preached and sung.

What was once denounced as presumption is now acknowledged to be the natural right of every child. Surely, if God be Father, it is reasonable to expect that He will assure His children of their parentage. It is the very first thing a child is taught to know. The knowledge is necessary to the child. Uncertainty secures no good purpose, and does much harm. It fills the heart with perplexity, suspicion, and resentment. It destroys filial instinct, and robs sonship of its inspiration, affection, and joy. Instead of keeping the soul humble, it turns it sour. God seeks the love of sons, not the service of slaves. If God speaks of anything to man He must speak of this. His nature demands it, for love must speak; the rights of sonship require it; and so, "And because ye are sons, God hath sent forth the Spirit of his Son into your hearts, crying, Abba, Father."[3] The Weslyans hailed the Spirit's cry with a glorious

---

[3] Galatians 4:6

shout of praise.

❧ Christian Perfection ❧

Still more distinctive was Wesley's teaching of Christian Perfection. Its accent was very marked. He preached it, expounded it, defended it, and insisted upon it continually. It laid him open to scurrilous attack and scandalous misrepresentation, but he never wavered. Its statement was the greatest work of his life, and its literature his unique contribution to the doctrines of the Church. He escaped many perils common to definitions by confining himself to scriptural expressions. Writing on the subject in 1769, he said, "By Christian Perfection I mean -- (1) Loving God with all our heart; (2) A heart and life all devoted to God; (3) Regaining the whole image of God; (4) Having all the mind that was in Christ; (5) Walking uniformly as Christ walked. If anyone means anything more or anything less by perfection, I have no concern with it."[4]

He wrote A Plain Account of Christian Perfection[5], which is to this day unsurpassed, if not unrivaled, as a statement and defense of the doctrine. It is a great testimony to his sanity, caution, and scriptural fidelity that, after a century and a half of Christian progress, nothing has been added, nor has any defect been discovered in his teaching upon the subject. His steady, clear light is still the best guide to the Canaan of perfect love. In this, as in everything else, he

---

[4] John Wesley's Journal, June 26, 1769
[5] See, Defining Biblical Holiness, Apprehending Truth Publishers.

was a man of action. He inquired of all his preachers, regularly, whether they had received the gift of perfect love. If their testimony was not very clear the question was followed by another: "Are you groaning after it?" In the Societies it was the same. Everywhere he inquired if believers were living in the enjoyment of entire sanctification. Nothing less was sufficient. Even new converts were urged to seek full salvation, the deliverance from the very presence of inbred sin. He observed that where the blessing was neglected the cause languished. The entire sanctification of believers was followed by the conversion of the ungodly.

On this subject the Weslyan Hymn-book is the best guide to the doctrine. The hymns classed under the heading, "Seeking for Full Redemption," are probably unique in the hymnology of the Church. They throb with the holiest aspirations of the soul, and pulsate with the indwelling life of God. As Paul's prayers are the best exposition of his theology, so these Weslyan hymns are the best exponents of the Weslyan doctrine. Selection is difficult in such profusion, but here is one:

> O come, and dwell in me,
> Spirit of power within!
> And bring the glorious liberty
> From sorrow, fear and sin.
>
> The seed of sin's disease,
> Spirit of health, remove,
> Spirit of finished holiness,

Spirit of perfect love.

Hasten the joyful day
Which shall my sins consume,
When old things shall be passed away,
And all things new become.

The original offense
Out of my soul erase;
Enter Thyself, and drive it hence,
And take up all the place.

In those lines is the very kernel of the Weslyan conception of scriptural holiness. Here is another:

O grant that nothing in my soul
May dwell, but Thy pure love alone;
O may Thy love possess me whole,

My joy, my treasure, and my crown!
Strange flames far from my heart remove,
My every act, word, thought, be love.

This blessing was declared to be the gift of God through faith, and wrought in the soul by the sanctifying spirit of truth. It is not of works, any more than pardon is of works. It is not by striving, any more than peace is by striving. It is preceded by conviction, and received through faith. The act of claiming is set forth in lines familiar to every Weslyan:

Saviour, to Thee my soul looks up,
My present Saviour Thou!
In all the confidence of hope,
I claim the blessing now.

'Tis done! Thou dost this moment save,
With full salvation bless;
Redemption through Thy blood I have,
And spotless love and peace.

This is the scriptural holiness Wesley declared Weslyans were raised up to spread through the land. This is the gospel he preached; a gospel of present, free, universal salvation; a gospel of assured acceptance in the love of God; a gospel of complete deliverance from all inward and outward sin; a gospel of grace so perfect, that the whole life is maintained in the will of God. Its accent was in the greatness of man's need, and the sufficiency of God's grace in Christ Jesus.

❧ The Influence of the Weslyan Revival ❧

It is impossible to trace the influence of the gospel or to gauge its revolutionary power in the world. It began a new era. It quickened the churches, changed the constitution of England, permeated the life of America, carried blessings to the Colonies, freed the slave and inaugurated the missionary enterprise which is destined to save the world. The Evangelical

Revival saved England by bringing new conceptions of God, new ideas of religion, new estimates of manhood, a new sense of responsibility and a baptism of

> *The character of a people's God is reflected in the life and institutions of the nation.*

power by which ideals could be transmuted into life. No nation can be better than its God. Like God, like people! The character of a people's God is reflected in the life and institutions of the nation. Religion is the formative and dominant power. The fundamental distinctions of races are religious. Every problem is at the root a religious problem. Wesley found England in the grip of the doctrines of election and predestination. Calvinism did reverent homage to the sovereignty of God, and it produced saints of mighty power; but it emphasized God to the neglect of man. Its sovereignty became arbitrary, meretricious, and almost capricious, until it was a caricature of the God and Father of Jesus Christ. The Calvinism of ecclesiasticism had a corresponding Calvinism in secular and national life. The few were elect, the rest were reprobate. The elect monopolized the privileges; the rest existed to be their hewers of wood and drawers of water. Election was not according to merit, but by birth and favor. The elect possessed all things. They had all the land, all the wealth, all the votes, all the learning, and everything else worth having in the nation. A democratic gospel changed all that. The Evangelical Revival carried everywhere a gospel of equality before God. The revival saved the land from revolution. "The man in the street" got the Weslyan conception of Christianity, with the result that national life has been remodeled on the pattern of Weslyan doctrine. The whole march of progress for more than a century has been a succession of reforms, breaking up monopolies, destroying high fences, and bringing the life of the nation into line with the new conception of the kingdom of heaven. True it is that other forces have been at work. Scientific discoveries, economic developments, and industrial organizations have done their part; but the result is due more to the revival that sought man as man and judged him apart from the accidents of birth and possessions, than to anything else. It let loose the dynamic, and led the way to the goal. The archetype of a Christian nation's life is the government of heaven, and there, helplessness is the first claim, manhood the supreme value, and righteousness the first law.

The doctrines of the Weslyan are now heard in all the churches. All preach the universal gospel, all evangelicals accept the doctrine of Assurance, and the teaching concerning holiness is as zealously taught at Keswick as at City Road. But the mission of Weslyanism is needed now as much as ever. The wider acceptance of doctrine cannot compensate for the loss of intensity, and the spread of the truth does not always carry with it a corresponding zeal. It is possible to be evangelical without being evangelistic. There is still the same need to seek the lost. In the developments of religious thought the center has been shifted from individual salvation to social condition. Wesley made no such blunder, and there is need for his successors to stand in the old paths. The wider belief in the possibility of assurance has been accompanied by other teaching, which has weakened rather than intensified the experience. Testimony is needed. Abstract truth can never take the place of the living witness. Let the children of Wesley speak openly in clear and certain speech. Scriptural holiness is not yet spread through the land. There are thousands in the churches who have not so much as heard of perfect love as a present possession. The sons of Wesley have a great heritage and a great responsibility. God has wrought great things by them, but greater tasks await them. There are many adversaries. There are perils in the remembrance of the past, and perils in the aspirations for the future. But the God that raised can keep and guide. He is not only the Father of the Wesleys, He is the God and Father of our Lord Jesus Christ, who is head over all things to His Church. The lineage goes beyond Wesley to Pentecost. Weslyanism is in the hands of the living Spirit. If, under His blessing, the commemoration be kept, the Ebenezer will become an altar, the starting point of a deeper devotion and a larger service, in which all the nations of the earth shall be blessed. The gospel which made the democracy is the only gospel by which the democracy can be saved. There lies the opportunity and responsibility of Weslyanism. There Weslyanism will find her conquest or her grave.

> Light of life, seraphic Fire,
> Love divine! Thyself impart;
> Every fainting soul inspire,
> Shine in every drooping heart.
>
> Every mournful sinner cheer,

Scatter all our guilty gloom,
Son of God, appear, appear!
To Thy human temples come.

Come in this accepted hour;
Bring Thy heavenly kingdom in;
Fill us with the glorious power,
Rooting out the seeds of sin.

Nothing more can we require,
We will covet nothing less;
Be Thou all our heart's desire,
All our joy, and all our peace!

The Doctrine of Christian Perfection

It was the settled conviction of John Wesley that the Lord had raised up the Weslyan people "to spread Scriptural Holiness throughout the land." The doctrine was in a peculiar sense committed to them. Perhaps it would not be quite true to say it was discovered by them, but they received it, preached it, and formulated it in their teaching as never before in the history of the Christian Church. The witness to the experience has come down through the ages, but John Wesley became its apostle. For thirty years he preached it, expounded it, and defended it. When he died, he deposited it with the Weslyan people as their special charge and responsibility. A collection of his teachings, warnings, and appeals on this subject would come with a shock to many of the people called Weslyans. If it were not for Wesley's Hymn-book, there would be many who had not so much as heard of the doctrine. The late Dr. Dale used to say that the last word on the subject was still with Wesley, but he was equally sure the last word had not yet been spoken. He regretted that the Weslyan people had done nothing to develop the doctrine. Keswick has tried to correct the Weslyan emphasis by stating the doctrine from the Calvinistic angle, and some American theologians have attempted its statement in modern terms; but the standard teaching is still that of Wesley.

❧ The Need For Restatement ❧

Wesley's statement of the doctrine was obviously incomplete, but had it been complete it would have needed a new birth for the new age. Truth needs to be reborn. Words change their content, and lose their value. Some become archaic, and others obsolete. Truth must be progressive. New problems call for new developments. Faith must speak in new tongues, if it would cast out devils and heal the diseases and wounds of the world. There were some things upon which even Wesley hesitated to pronounce. I love the frankness with which he dismissed what he could not explain: "I confess that I cannot split this hair." His teaching was experimental, and he refused to be entangled in philosophical speculations. He never shirked a practical problem, but he could only deal with those of his own age. Principles are eternal and universal, but rules are determined by times and circumstances. His anxiety to avoid all suspicion of preaching "a sinless perfection" led him to reckon in the category of sins some infirmities and limitations which are entirely destitute of moral character. It is never satisfactory to have a problem dismissed with a gesture, as when in 1776 he answers the question, "Is it sinless?" with the remark, "It is not worth while to contend for a term: it is salvation from sin." The contention is for something more than a term. It is a demand for clearness of thought, intelligence of faith, and instruction in the implications of experience.

We have to plead guilty to the charge that we have not been faithful stewards of this great "depositum" of grace. There is with one consent a culpable silence on the subject. For sixteen years I heard candidates for ordination asked if they ever preached specifically and definitely on the subject of Holiness as an experience, and the answer was always the same. All their preaching was on Holiness, but they had not specifically expounded or urged the experience.

⊷ Causes For Neglect ⊶

The causes for neglect are numerous and various. No doubt some avoid it because of its demands. They are content with the measure of light they have, because they are satisfied with the level at which they live. Others are in bondage to prejudice. The logic of unbelief is the same in saints as in sinners. The ungodly reject

> *The logic of unbelief is the same in saints as in sinners.*

the Christian religion because of its hypocrites, and the saints reject the doctrine because of its caricatures. Saintliness has stiffened into types, and they dislike the mold. The profession of the experience has exhibited a severity, complacency, and censoriousness which are peculiarly repellent. Perfection has been too often associated with the phylacteries of the Pharisee to make it commendable. Everyone admits that no cause should be judged by its counterfeit, but in religion the counterfeit keeps many from seeking the true.

❧ I Have Seen an End of All Perfection ❧

A more serious factor has been that for two generations the thought of the age has been hostile. The idea of evolution has been dominant. There has been no place for the supernatural or the catastrophic. It has been assumed that all life must advance in orderly sequence. Salvation must be by culture. There was no need for the Second Birth, and the Second Blessing was an outrage and an offense. The man was in the child, and in the natural man there was latent all the qualities of spiritual life. Clever people asked ignorant questions. If a Second Blessing, why not a thirty-second? If Perfect, how can progress be possible? If saved from sin, why pray the Lord's Prayer? If saved to the uttermost, what is there beyond? If Love is made perfect, what comes of discipline, ethical values, and the militant character of discipleship?

That tyranny is past. Naturalistic evolution as a universal law of life is discredited and abandoned. The fact of conversion is psychologically sound. The experience of a Second Crisis is no longer counted foolish in the wisdom of this world. We ask no patronage from the mentality of the learned, but we welcome an attitude of mind that is sympathetic to spiritual truth.

The witness still suffers from inadequate statement. It is quite likely that it always will. For it must be remembered that the experience is often received by persons unskilled in the art of precise expression. Philip's testimony was at fault in two points out of five, and there are many disciples less skilled than he. There are witnesses to the fact of experience, but they are not able to define and explain. They have never acquired the habit of mental analysis, nor have they the knowledge required for exactness of definition. Happily, grace is not conditioned by theology. These things are hid from the clever and the vain, but they are revealed unto babes.

The literature upon the subject is singularly disappointing. I have for years urged the young biblical scholars of the ministry to explore and restate the teaching of the Scriptures on the subject of Holiness. I hope some of them are doing it. I am sure it must be done, for while the witness may be sincere, the teaching is confused, unrelated, and incomplete. The Bible is every man's best guide, but teaching is necessary, otherwise God would not have included teachers among His gifts to the Church. Wesley is often commended for his sagacity in defining the doctrine in terms of Scripture, and for the purposes of controversy it was proof of his wisdom. For instruction in the faith something more is needed than to be told that: "Pure love alone, reigning in the heart, is the whole of Christian Perfection." So it is. No words could set before the mind a higher ideal, a simpler principle, or a greater incentive; but there is something in the general terms that engenders vagueness of conception and non-ethical emotion. Faith needs to be instructed, and the heart must be able to give reasons for its experience and hope. Christian teachers must translate their theology into the speech of the twentieth century.

❧ The Need For Revival ❧

Revival is more important than re-statement. Testimony to the possession of the blessing is exceedingly rare. To our fathers there was given a witness of the Spirit to a definite gift as distinct as that borne to adoption. God's ambassadors are witnesses as well as messengers. What has come to our testimony? In how many pulpits is it heard throughout the year? What about the classmeeting? Testimony is impossible without experience assured to the heart. Failure in fellowship has its roots far deeper than the changes in social life. What about the theological training of the ministry? Is the doctrine expounded with clearness, and the experience urged upon those who are to be the future leaders of our Israel? Is there not occasion to ask whether the doctrine is any longer believed and taught among us?

> God of eternal truth and grace,
> Thy faithful promise seal!
> Thy word, Thy oath, to Abraham's race,
> In us, e'en us, fulfill.

> Let us, to perfect love restored,
> Thy image here retrieve,
> And in the presence of our Lord
> The life of angels live.

> That mighty faith on me bestow
> Which cannot ask in vain,

The Call to Christian Perfection

Which holds, and will not let Thee go,
Till I my suit obtain.

Till Thou into my soul inspire
Thy perfect love unknown,
And tell my infinite desire,
"Whate'er Thou wilt, be done."

But is it possible that I
Should live and sin no more?
Lord, if on Thee I dare rely,
The faith shall bring the power.

On me the faith divine bestow
Which doth the mountain move;
And all my spotless life shall show
The omnipotence of love.

What Christian Perfection Implies

Much of the difficulty in the subject of Christian Perfection lies in the ambiguity which clings to the word "perfect." It is used with various meanings, both in the Scriptures and in common speech. In everyday talk, common sense is allowed to interpret the significance of the word. When we speak of a child as perfect, we are not foolish enough to quibble over the finality of its perfection. Unfortunately, common sense seldom gets a chance in theology. We quarrel over terms and tenses, abstract definitions and speculative hypotheses, till we cannot see the wood for trees. There is no absolute perfection but in God. All other perfection is relative. There is a perfection that is initial, a perfection that is progressive, and a perfection that is final. The Apostle Paul was perfect, even when he had not yet attained to perfection. There is neither contradiction nor confusion in the two statements, except to the man who is himself confused.

Paul declared emphatically in Philippians 3:12 that he was not perfect. Perfection was a goal he was striving to attain, but he did not expect to reach it in this life. That is the perfection that appeals. The fact is overlooked that in verse 15 he includes himself among the perfect. Here is a paradox that cannot be relegated to the number of Wesley's unsplittable hairs. St. Paul, in the same paragraph, repudiates perfection, and claims to be perfect. Those who reason by the rule-of-thumb method argue that both statements cannot be true, and that the emphatic personal word is conclusive. The Apostle made no claim to the perfect, and the second statement must be ruled by the first. Truth is generally expressed in a paradox, and in a paradox two statements apparently contradict each other, but the contradiction is only apparent. There is a fundamental unity of which the statements are the complimentary expression. It is true, for instance, that no man hath seen God at any time, but it is also true that the pure in heart see God. Both are true. So it is with perfection. It is obviously true that there is a perfection to which no one has attained, or can attain, either in this life or the next. Perfection belongs to God. For man there is a perfection for which he is apprehended in Christ, to which he cannot come until grace is consummated in glory. That is the perfection St. Paul had not attained. On the other hand there is a perfection that is both commanded and promised.

It is many years since I set myself to a scientific and earnest study of the New Testament on this subject. I had entered into an experience that I could neither define nor defend. I had to find reasons for the assurance of which I had no doubt. Books did not help me. I had no skill in Bible study, but with patient humility and much prayer I was led gradually into the light. I found in the Scriptures more than one angle of presentation for the same experience. The legal aspect expressed it in terms of law. The Temple had a different vocabulary from the Law Court. Neither was complete without the other. The family completed both the Court and the Temple. Perfection in the Court was acquittal without condemnation. Perfection in the Temple was purity without defect, cleanness without stain. Perfection in the family was the perfection of love.

There is therefore no condemnation to them that are in Christ Jesus: THE LAW. The Blood of Jesus Christ His Son cleanseth us from all sin: THE TEMPLE. Herein is our love made perfect. There is no fear in love; but perfect love casteth out fear: THE HOME.

No interpretation of Perfection is complete that ignores any one of these three angles of interpretation.

❧ Finality or Fitness ❧

I shall never forget the excitement with which I discovered another word for Perfection. The word for the Perfection that is final is teleios[1]. That is the big word for Perfection. It is used of Christ and His redeeming work which is all Perfect. It is used also of the ultimate consummation of Grace, and of perfect development. The word I discovered was katartizo[2], which does not mean the finality of a thing, but its fitness. The uses of the word are illuminating. It is used of mending nets (Matt. 4:21); to set in order as in music (Matt.

---

[1] GK 5048 – τελειόω
[2] GK 2675 – καταρτίζω

21:16); to fit into perfect relationship (1 Cor. 1:10); to adjust that which is dislocated (Gal. 6:1); to complete that which is lacking (1 Thess. 3:10); to frame together various parts of a machine (Heb. 11:3). There is nothing very difficult to understand in this kind of perfection. Mending is done to repair damage and make fit again for use. Perfecting music is so arranging it that all discords are lost in the perfection of harmony. Limbs fitly joined work together in the unity of the body. No one objects to perfection in the joints of arms, legs, and necks. Putting into joint a dislocated limb is making it perfect. The various parts of creation are perfectly fitted and framed together. When that which is lacking is supplied, the defective is made perfect. Three pence added to nine pence make a perfect shilling. That is what is meant by perfection. It is complete deliverance from everything that makes the soul unfit for, and unequal to, the will of God; the adjustment of life to perfect harmony, and the adaptation of all its powers to the purpose of God; and the supply of all grace, wisdom, power, and whatever else is lacking for efficient obedience to every demand in the fellowship of God in Christ. It is life so completely saved that there is no defect, no disorder, no discord.

❧ What Man Lost in Adam ❧

Nothing is more obvious than the anxiety of exponents of Christian Perfection to keep down the standard of attainment. It is the rebound from all kinds of fanaticism, ignorance, and immortality. The doctrine needs to be safeguarded, but its best defense is in the heights. Negations are not strongholds. Enthusiasm cannot be kindled by contemplation of its limitations. We need the affirmations of truth and the confirmation of testimony. We are told that Christian Perfection is not angelic, and yet we pray, "Thy will be done, as in heaven, so on earth."[3]

Neither is it Adamic, and yet, it is putting on "the new man" which is "after the image of Him that created him."[4] There is evidently some confusion in these statements, for the salvation procured by Jesus Christ cannot be less than a complete restoration to man's original state of perfection. Indeed:

In Him the sons of Adam boast
More blessings than their father lost.

Redemption implies a restoration. Something forfeited is bought back; something lost is restored. What is the something that constituted man's original perfection, and which was lost through sin? The Scriptures make it plain that God made man upright. He came from the hands of his Maker a being of distinguished excellence and perfection. God made man in His own image, and after His own likeness. So far all evangelical believers agree, but when it is asked in what this image and perfection consist there is an end to agreement. The first chapters of Genesis are the paradise of all speculation. In the dim light truth takes shape according to

---

[3] Luke 11:2
[4] Ephesians 4:24; Colossians 3:10

every man's fancy. By many the perfection of man in his original state has been greatly exaggerated. It cannot have been his physical nature that was made in the image of God; for "God is a Spirit." He had physical limitations and appetites that are still common to the race. Neither was his perfection in knowledge absolute. The woman sinned because she was deceived -- a fact that indicates a lack of intellectual penetration combined with moral perversity. So it was not in knowledge perfection lay. His nature was endowed with such powers as made intercourse with spirits possible. He had fellowship with God, and was accessible to Satan. His perfection was spiritual and moral, held on condition of obedience, and exposed to moral and spiritual assault. When man sinned he forfeited his inheritance. He lost God. The sense of the Divine presence and approval vanished. Losing God, he lost life. The soul that sinneth dies. The death of the soul does not mean extinction. It is the loss of that spiritual consciousness in which all right direction and control of man's various faculties and powers have their source. In spiritual death no part of man's nature is destroyed, but every part becomes disordered and deranged. In the life of sin God is dethroned, and the lust of the eye, the lust of the flesh, and the pride of life hold sway over the soul.

❧ The Extent of Recovery in Christ ❧

The essential elements in man's loss through sin are the sense of divine fellowship and moral power to live in harmony with the divine will. Other results followed, but they stand to these as effect to cause, and will be remedied as man is restored. The curse upon the world will be lifted as man is redeemed. God's concern is with men. One of the things frequently forgotten is that man's sin made no difference in the requirements of the moral law. There was no lowering of the standard. The laws of the moral realm are inherent in the divine character, and as unalterable as the laws of Nature. Obedience can never be vicarious, in the sense that it releases another from obligation to obey. "Justification by faith is not a legal fiction, but a moral anticipation." The end of grace is to make sinful men holy. Grace comes to condemn sin in the flesh "That the righteousness of the law might be fulfilled in us, who walk not after the flesh, but after the Spirit." (Rom. 8:4). Man's duty is not changed. God asked of Adam no more than that he should love Him with all his heart, soul, mind, and strength and of us He demands nothing less. The moral law is not repealed in grace. It is not the condition of salvation, but it is the rule and standard of life. Love is not a substitute for righteousness; it is the filling of the law. Salvation restores the soul to peace and fellowship with God, and so renews the nature and sustains the heart, as to enable man to live according to the divine will.

> *The moral law is not repealed in grace.*

❧ Made Perfect ❧

It does not lift man above the possibility of temptation, for both Adam and Jesus suffered being tempted. Neither can it bring immunity from frailty, limitation, and ignorance, for humanity is sanctified without being absorbed. It cannot be final for it is still probationary. The writer to the Hebrews prayed that they might be made "perfect in every good work to do his will." The prayer is the best definition. It is a restoration of relationship, a renewal of nature, a sufficiency of grace that makes it possible to live in all things according to the will of God. It is a prayer for restored fitness and power, in which His purpose shall be fulfilled. Christian Perfection is a question of Christian efficiency. We are the workmanship of a Perfect Worker, and it would be strange if perfection were impossible to us in Him.

> He wills that I should holy be,
> That holiness I long to feel;
> That full divine conformity
> To all my Saviour's righteous will.

> See, Lord, the travail of Thy soul
> Accomplished in the change of mine,
> And plunge me, every whit made whole,
> In all the depths of love divine.

> On Thee, O God, my soul is stayed,
> And waits to prove Thine utmost will;
> The promise, by Thy mercy made,
> Thou canst, Thou wilt, in me fulfill.

> Now let Thy Spirit bring me in,
> And give Thy servant to possess

What Christian Perfection Implies

The land of rest from inbred sin,
The land of perfect holiness.

Lord, I believe Thy power the same,
The same Thy truth and grace endure;
And in Thy blessed hands I am,
And trust Thee for a perfect cure.
Come, Saviour, come, and make me whole!
Entirely all my sins remove;
To perfect health restore my soul,
To perfect holiness and love.

The Essential Element in Christian Perfection

The essential principle of all moral evil is alienation of the heart from God. "The carnal mind is enmity against God."[1] This enmity is the source of all the streams of evil. There can be no redemption except by the healing of this spring. Whatever relationships need readjustment the heart must be cleansed. There is no substitute for a clean heart. Till this is accomplished, nothing is done; when this is done all things become possible. The putting right of the inward principle and the cleansing of the springs of thought and desire, motive and will, must of necessity rectify the entire character, transform the whole life, and reconstruct all its relationships. This is the work of the gospel. It reconciles man to God, slays the principle of enmity, and sheds abroad the love of God in the heart. In Jesus Christ God's favor is restored to man, and God's love is begotten in his soul. Few people would be found to dissent from Wesley's statement, "Pure love alone, reigning in the heart and life, this is the whole of Christian perfection."

Yet for more than fifty years he was in continual controversy over it, and controversy always leads to definition

[1] Romans 8:7

and testing. Throughout the whole period he never varied. Through all explanations he clave to the same simple statements, and in all defense he held to the same essentials. There is no more remarkable example of consistency in the history of doctrinal discussion. One of his earliest definitions states it to mean, "Salvation from all sin, and loving God with all the heart"[2]; and one of his latest defines it as "a full deliverance from all sin, and a renewal in the whole image of God."[3] Objection was taken to the term "Perfection." He contended that the word is scriptural, and therefore he says, "Neither you nor I can in conscience object to it, unless we would send the Holy Ghost to school, and teach Him to speak who made the tongue."[4] He would not drop the word, but he took great pains to explain it. "By 'perfection' I mean perfect love, or the loving of God with all our heart, so as to rejoice evermore, to pray without ceasing, and in everything to give thanks."[5]

What is the objection to this teaching? Is it not Scriptural? Is it not stated in the very language of Scripture? He himself says, "This perfection cannot be a delusion unless the Bible be a delusion too."[6] Was he mistaken, and a preacher of a false doctrine? Or have we forsaken the Word of the Lord?

The sanctification of man's nature is a work of love. Its

---

[2] John Wesley's Journal, May 4, 1765. From a note referenced to January 1, 1733.
[3] Expressed in a letter to John Ogilvie, August 7, 1785
[4] From a letter addressed to Mrs. Penelope Maitland, May 12, 1763
[5] From a letter addressed to Elizabeth Hardy, April 5, 1758.
[6] From a letter addressed to Lawrence Coughlan, August 27, 1768.

progress is in the development of the principle of love, and entire sanctification consists in the perfection of love in the heart and life.

ꙮ The Whole Law ꙮ

Love sums up the whole of the Christian religion. Without love nothing counts. Knowledge, beneficence, and faith are nothing without love. The greatest gifts, including prophecy and miraculous powers, are nothing without love. It comprehends all God's revelation of Himself, for God is love. It sums up all man's duty. All the Commandments are comprehended in this, "Thou shalt love the Lord thy God with all thy heart, and with all thy soul, and with all thy strength, and with all thy mind; and thy neighbour as thyself."[7] There has never been any other commandment. Love is, and always has been, the fulfilling of the law. Mechanical obedience of the letter never could have satisfied God. There are two covenants, but they declare one kind of righteousness, and that righteousness is the perfect love of God and our neighbor. These two great demands of the Divine Law are universal and eternal, equally binding in all worlds and in all ages. Just as in tracing back existence we come to the necessity of God's being, so, in tracing back principles, we come to the necessity of God's character. The Law is not a principle of Nature, nor a matter of creation for the government of the world; it is inherent in the divine character, coexistent and coeternal with the divine nature. The obligation to be holy is in the fact of

---

[7] Luke 10:27

His holiness, and the demand for love is inherent in the fact that God is love. "Ye shall be holy; for I am holy."[8] Love is the fulfilling of the law; not its substitute. It keeps the commandments and sinneth not. The gospel is the power of God unto salvation. It saves from the power and pollution of sin. This is its one grand result: "The blood of Jesus Christ, His Son, cleanseth us from all sin."[9] Into the cleansed soul there comes to abide the Spirit of God, the fruit of whose presence is the love of God permeating every part of heart and life. Love reigns supreme. Christian perfection is this gift of love made perfect in the soul.

❧ Love Made Perfect ❧

Whether a man's love is perfect is a question that must rest with his own consciousness and his God. The heart is known to no one else. The most palpable failure to attain to a high standard may not be inconsistent with the most ardent devotion, and on the other hand one who is "as touching the law blameless" may be destitute of love. The question of fact can be settled only by testimony, but the proof of the testimony is the "fruit unto holiness" by which it is sustained. There are many artificial tests which tend to neutralize the testimony. The only authorized test of love is obedience. Love that runs to license is of the flesh, and not of God. There have been many intelligent witnesses to the gift of perfecting grace. Thousands of sane and saintly people have borne witness to a

---

[8] Leviticus 11:44,45; 19:2; 20:7,26; 1 Peter 1:16
[9] 1 John 1:7

definite experience in which they have received an assurance of love perfected in the soul, and a gift of power that has lifted life into a new plane of fellowship and power. Their lives have triumphed over evil, and overflowed in love and joy. There are thousands, on the other hand, who are equally sure their hearts are not clean, neither is their love perfect. They are conscious not only of failure, but of guilt. They know that their hearts ought to be pure, and their love ought to be perfect, and what ought to be can be. God never commands what He cannot enable. He makes possible whatever He demands.

✎ Love Not Yet Perfect ✎

In what sense may the love of God be imperfect in the soul? A thing may be perfect in quality and defective in quantity. An article may be up to standard and of short measure. Again, a thing may be perfect, though not yet perfected. There is a difference between initial and final perfection. The two "perfects" in Philippians 3 are a good example of this

> *The capacity for love expands with the exercise of love.*

distinction. Perfect love is not an end, but a beginning. It is love without corruption, without flaw, without deficiency. It has to do with quantity rather than quality. God's love is something more than a gift out of His treasury; it is the gift of Himself. Love and God are one. "God is love; and he that dwelleth in love dwelleth in God, and God in him. Herein is our love made perfect."[10] That is the secret of it all. Love is

---

[10] 1 John 4:16, 17

made perfect by the abiding fullness of the Divine Presence. Self dies in the soul filled with God. Love reigns where He abides. The capacity for love expands with the exercise of love, but perfect love always fills to the utmost limit. A teacup may be as full as a bucket, and God fills the surrendered soul to the full.

❧ When? ❧

On the testimony of many witnesses this experience may come suddenly upon the simple exercise of faith. And why not? There is nothing inconceivable or inconsistent in the statement that the Lord may come suddenly to His Temple, and fill it with His glory. The cleansing of the heart is by faith, and there is nothing to hinder faith from operating suddenly and immediately. God's promise waits our claim. His power has no conditions but our consent. His presence stays for nothing but the open door. He waits to save to the uttermost even now.

> O Jesus, at Thy feet we wait,
> Till Thou shalt bid us rise,
> Restor'd to our unsinning state,
> To love's sweet paradise.
>
> Saviour from sin, we Thee receive;
> From all indwelling sin,
> Thy blood, we steadfastly believe,
> Shall make us throughly clean.

Since Thou wouldst have us free from sin,
And pure as those above,
Make haste to bring Thy nature in,
And perfect us in love.

The counsel of Thy love fulfill;
Come quickly, gracious Lord!
Be it according to Thy will,
According to Thy word!

According to our faith in Thee
Let it to us be done;
O that we all Thy face might see,
And know as we are known!

O that the perfect grace were given,
The love diffused abroad!
O that our hearts were all a heaven,
For ever filled with God!

Christian Perfection as Interpreted by John Wesley

Wesley's theology was experimental. His statements were formulated from experience. He had no stereotyped forms, no rigid creed, no sense of finality. His message enlarged with years, and to the end he did not hesitate to correct his theological views. Less capacious minds stereotype their opinions, and are careful only to maintain them. Such can never be charged with inconsistency. Progress involves correction, and it is easy to quote the man who grows against himself. Further, Wesley was a practical theologian. His life was lived in a perpetual hurricane of controversy and incessant activity. He had no leisure for abstract speculation. Like the Apostle Paul, he was an evangelist first, and only incidentally a philosopher and a theologian. His wine-skins were always bursting. One after another the boundaries of creed and ecclesiasticism were swept away. He formulated no creed; elaborated no system. The standards of doctrine he left are embedded in sermons and expository notes. His system of Church government is embodied in a legal document, designed to secure the property to his people and the fellowship of his spiritual children. The completeness and consistency of his doctrine and discipline are due to the simplicity and transparency of the man. His principles were well and truly laid; and he had learned to distinguish between principles and opinions, things eternal and unchanging, and those which are temporary and provisional. For half a century he was stating, restating, and defending the doctrine of scriptural holiness. He examined thousands who professed to have entered into the experience. He himself testified to its possession, and for years contended that the Weslyan people were raised up to be its exponents and witnesses, and to spread it through the land.

❧ Wesley's Insistent Preaching of the Doctrine ❧

He preached it as an immediate, instantaneous, assured work of grace through faith. By it the believer is delivered from inbred sin. "Not by a slow and insensible growth in grace, but by the power of the Highest overshadowing you, in a moment, in the twinkling of an eye, so as utterly to abolish sin, and to renew you in His whole image! If you are simple of heart, if you are willing to receive the heavenly gift as a little child, without reasoning, why may you not receive it now?"[1] The seal of many witnesses confirmed his teaching. The plain fact is this: he was able to say, "I know many who love God with all their heart, mind, soul and strength. He is their one desire, their one delight, and they are continually happy in Him. They love their neighbor as themselves. They rejoice evermore, pray without ceasing, and

---

[1] From a letter addressed to Mary Cooke, September 24, 1785.

in everything give thanks. This is plain, sound, scriptural experience; and of this we have more and more living witnesses."[2] These were the seals to his preaching and the crown of his rejoicing. "I declared to all, 'We are saved from sin, we are made holy by faith.' This I testified in private, in public, in print; and God confirmed it by a thousand witnesses."[3]

Wesley insisted on all his preachers expounding, and explicitly urging, this doctrine of Full Salvation. Writing to Adam Clarke on November 26, 1790, on the doctrine, he says: "If we can prove that any of our local preachers, or leaders, either directly or indirectly, speak against it, let him be a local preacher or leader no longer. I doubt whether he should continue in society. Because he that could speak thus in our congregation cannot be an honest man."

There were declensions and periods of stagnation in his day. To what did he trace them, and what was his remedy? Of one society he says:

"I was surprised to find fifty members fewer than I left in October last. One reason is, Christian Perfection has been little insisted on; and where this is not done, be the preachers ever so eloquent, there is little increase, either in the number or grace of the hearers."[4]

He testifies again and again that, where Christian Perfection is not strongly, clearly, explicitly, and earnestly preached, the work of God declines. The devil hates the

---

[2] From a letter addressed to Elizabeth Hardy, December 26, 1761
[3] From a letter addressed to "Dear Lady", June 19, 1771
[4] John Wesley's Journal, September 30, 1765

doctrine, but God, in a remarkable way, crowns it with blessing. "Only do not forget," he says, "strongly and explicitly to urge believers to 'go on to perfection.' When this is constantly and earnestly done, the Word is always clothed with power[5] ... Till you press the believers to expect full salvation now, you must not look for any revival.[6]"

❧ The Charge of Perfectionism ❧

In nothing was Wesley so bitterly assailed as for his teaching of Christian Perfection. It cost him some of his most valued friends, and exposed him to all sorts of calumny and misrepresentation. His doctrine was attacked from opposite sides. Some objected that he placed the standard too high. The Calvinists charged him with making void the gospel of faith, because he insisted upon inward cleansing from all sin and a life in which the love of God reigns supreme. He demanded nothing less than obedience to all the commandments of God -- not only some of them, or most of them, but all of them -- from the least to the

> *It is his glory and joy to run in the way of God's commandments.*

greatest. "Whatever God has forbidden, he avoids; whatever God has enjoined, he does. It is his glory and joy to run in the way of God's commandments; it is his daily crown of rejoicing to do the will of God on earth, as it is done in heaven."[7] This is Wesley's standard of perfection. To this day the attack is

---

[5] From a letter addressed to Peard Dickinson, June 5, 1787
[6] From a letter addressed to Mr. Merryweather, of Yarm, February 8, 1766
[7] Wallace, J.L. (Ed.)., Wesley, J., Mahan, A. (2011) *Defining Biblical Holiness* (p.32), Brookfield, Missouri: Apprehending Truth Publishers.

41

maintained by the representatives of the Calvinistic faith. There are some conventions for the promotion of godliness where it is always in the background of their teaching. Eradication of inward sin is held to be impossible in this life. Subjugation is all we may hope for. Perfectionism is assailed as deadly heresy. The old questions of Wesley's day reappear in modern form. If salvation from sin means that Christians live without sin, what need will the sanctified have of the atoning blood? Such objections seem to regard the death of Christ as making up the balance of human merit before God, and to regard some sin in the heart as necessary to secure the peculiar value of the atoning blood. To make the death of Christ an occasion of release from perfect obedience comes very near to making the Cross the minister of sin.

❧ The Charge of Antinomianism ❧

Opposition comes also from the other extreme. While some charge him with putting the standard too high, others contend he puts it too low, because he says that "no man is able to perform the service which the Adamic law requires," that "no man is obliged to perform it,"[8] that "we are not under the angelic or the Adamic law." On this subject there is certainly some ambiguity in Wesley's teaching. He declines to call Christian Perfection "sinless,"[9] and yet he insists that it is salvation from all sin. At one time he classes "errors resulting from unavoidable ignorance and weakness" as sins; and at

[8] Ibid., (p.84)
[9] Ibid., (p.62)

another time he speaks of them as sins improperly so-called. Theoretically he contends that while man is in a corruptible body he can never attain to Adamic or angelic perfection, while practically he tells us we can keep all the commandments and do the will of God as it is done in heaven.

There is need for elucidation and co-ordination of his teaching. The explanation will probably be found in an exaggerated view of Adam's original perfection; and, if one dare say it, a somewhat lax and popular use of the word "sin." Whatever the explanation, no one familiar with Wesley's teaching will charge him with making void the law. He never spoke of the law as having passed away, in any sense, but as ceremonial ordinance and a condition of justification. Salvation is by faith and not by the works of the law, but the perfect law remains in force as the standard of life and obedience. The law is immutable, universal, and eternal -- "a transcript of the divine nature." The law of love is not new. It is no lowering of the standard. It is the fulfilling of the law. Grace does not release from obedience; it empowers it.

☙ A Charge Upon All ☙

Christ Jesus came into the world to save sinners. The seat of sin is in the soul. It is neither in the physical nor intellectual powers. Christian Perfection is salvation from sin. A higher meaning than this it cannot have; a lower meaning it must not have. Sin defaced God's image in man, and turned his love to enmity. Jesus restores the image, and turns enmity to love. By Him provision is made that "the righteousness of the law might be fulfilled in us." The law is not a system of statutes to be mechanically observed, but a principle of love possible alike to angels and men: love filling the heart and reigning in the life is as possible to those of the highest intellectual attainments as to those of the lowest. The same commandment is laid upon all, and the same privilege of grace is open to all. If any man would know more of this subject, let him read John Wesley's *Plain Account of Christian Perfection*,[10] and above all, let him search the Scriptures that he may know the fullness of God's saving grace.

> What! never speak one evil word,
> Or rash, or idle, or unkind!
> O how shall I, most gracious Lord,
> This mark of true perfection find?
>
> Thy sinless mind in me reveal,
> Thy Spirit's plenitude impart;
> And all my spotless life shall tell
> The abundance of a loving heart.
>
> Saviour, I long to testify
> The fullness of Thy saving grace;
> O might Thy Spirit the blood apply,
> Which bought for me the sacred peace!
>
> Forgive, and make my nature whole,

---

[10] *Defining Biblical Holiness*, Apprehending Truth Publishers

My inbred malady remove;
To perfect health restore my soul,
To perfect holiness and love.

VI

Christian Perfection in Relation to Sins and Mistakes

St. John's teaching concerning sin settles some things for all time. Chapter 3 of his First Epistle emphatically declares:

1) That sin is lawlessness.
2) Jesus Christ was manifested to take away sins.
3) Whosoever is begotten of God, and abideth in Him, does not commit sin.
4) The difference between the children of God and the children of the devil is that one sins and the other does not. Nothing can be plainer than that. Every man born of God quits sin. If a man sins, he is not a child of God but a child of Satan.[1]

There is no escape from that alternative. He that is not with God is with the devil. It is often asserted that all are of God and none of the devil. God is the universal Father, and therefore every man is His child. Jesus did not so teach. When the Jews claimed God for their Father, Jesus denied the claim and declared them to be the children of the devil. They said "...

---

[1] 1 John 3:4, 5, 6, 8, 9

We have one Father, even God. Jesus said ... Ye are of your father, the devil" (John 8:41, 44). They claimed sonship with God through Abraham their father. They forgot that soul-relationships rest, not upon lineal descent, but on spiritual affinities. Spiritual kinship is not of blood, but of spirit. Though men belong by right to God they may be by choice the possession of the devil. No man is the devil's by any right of creation. He did not make us. We are the work of God's hands and the people of His pasture. Neither is any man the devil's by birth. We may have been born in sin and shapen in iniquity, but for all that we belong to God, not Satan. Whatever the power of heredity, it lays no such curse upon the child, and establishes no such right for the prince of darkness. Original sin is counterbalanced by original grace. No soul belongs to Satan either by any vestige of right or by any law of necessity. Neither is any man a child of God by reason of any of these things. The relationship of the creation is forfeited by sin. The sonship of the covenant avails only till moral responsibility is attained. The Timothys need to be born again as truly as the Ishmaels. No rite of baptism can secure it, neither is any man the Lord's any more than the devil's of necessity. Spiritual parentage is by adoption. There can be no adoption without consent. Therefore, choice settles sonship. In the spiritual realm every man chooses his own Father.

On the other hand, in the first chapter of the same Epistle John says:

"If we say that we have no sin, we deceive ourselves, and the truth is not in us."[2]

---

[2] 1 John 1:8

These passages present a real difficulty. They seem to absolutely contradictory, that if one be true the other must be false; and it is between these two statements we find the most contention. Some contend for the absolute deliverance of the soul from sin, and others for the inevitable continuance of sin in the soul.

❧ What is Sin? ❧

The explanation will be found in a complete study of St. John's treatment of the doctrine of sin. He defines it as lawlessness. It is not the violation of a commandment, but a principle of evil within the soul. Sin is not an act, but an attitude. Man is not so much a sinner because he is a transgressor, as he is a transgressor because he is a sinner. Its seat is neither in the body nor in the mind; it is in the heart. In the first chapter he exposes three false views of sin. If we deny the reality of sin under cloak of fellowship with God, we lie and do not the truth (1:6). If we deny our responsibility for sin, we deceive ourselves and the truth is not in us (1:8). If we deny the fact of sin and say we have not sinned, we make God a liar and His Word is not in us (1:10). None of these passages teach that sin must always be in us, or that we must inevitably keep on sinning. On the contrary, they make plain God's provision for sin. He pardons and cleanses those who confess their sins, and the blood of His Son cleanses from all sin those who walk in the light. Jesus Christ came to save sinners from sin, and He does what He came to do. "Whosoever abideth in him sinneth not: whosoever sinneth hath not seen him, neither known him."[3] "He that committeth sin is of the devil."[4]

This does not mean that the Christian can never again fall away into sin. All scripture -- John's writings included -- warns us that the child of God can fall into sin. God's saving power is conditioned on man's consent. What it does mean is that the whole attitude of the regenerate man is contrary to sin. He stands resolutely opposed to it. He antagonizes it. His nature is cleansed of that which hankered after it. He has been made partaker of the divine nature, and the bent of his nature is one with God's.

❧ Sins Improperly So Called ❧

This is a hard saying, and it is not a matter of surprise if even John Wesley's logic faltered in the presence of the persistent criticism to which it is obviously exposed. Christian perfection has been regarded as claiming, not only deliverance from sin, but from all error, limitation and defect. Such is manifestly impossible. Christian perfection is not infallibility. It does not deify men. It does not dehumanize humanity; it sanctifies it. A clean heart does not imply a perfect head.

> *Christian perfection is not infallibility.*

So long as we are in this world there will be unavoidable errors and imperfections of judgment. The mistake is in regarding such errors and imperfections as sins. The decalogue gives no pronouncement upon them. There is no explicit direction concerning them in either Old or New Testament.

[3] 1 John 3:6
[4] 1 John 3:8

The Word of God is the standard of both doctrine and conduct, but in neither does it systematize and codify its teaching. In doctrine it reveals truth through the records of history, and in conduct it lays down principles, not rules. For doctrine the Scriptures need to be searched. In conduct the principles are to be discovered and applied.

Wesley speaks of these errors as "deviations from the perfect law, and need an atonement." They are inevitable, and sometimes even unconscious; and yet he declares, whether "known or unknown, they need the atoning blood." In his sermon on "Perfection," however, he says they are improperly called sins, and adds, "The word sin is never taken in this sense in Scripture." There is no scriptural warrant regarding either physical infirmities, or mental weaknesses, or any of their proper consequences as sins. They are not sins. Such imperfections are utterly destitute of moral character. They require no repentance. No man can repent of an act which is the result of pure ignorance, or of something which was unavoidable. He may regret these things, but regret and repentance are by no means the same. Neither do they need atonement. Deliverance from mistakes is not by the blood of the Cross, but by the discipline of experience. This is a perfection that is by suffering, and not by faith.

❧ The Levitical Law and the Lord's Prayer ❧

The Levitical law required sacrifice for violations of the law committed in ignorance. This is the basis on which "unavoidable infirmities" are regarded as sins requiring atonement, but it proves too much. These sacrifices were for diseases, some of which were providentially inflicted. This standard would make motherhood a sin! It would include bricks and mortar among the things for which "atonement" had to be made (see Lev. 14:53). The new covenant has put away all these symbolical classifications. It is upon the heart that the perfect law is written, and it is in the heart that God perfects the love which is the fulfilling of the law. A mistake is a wrong act, in which the right was intended. Motive determines moral quality. Intention, not achievement, is the divine test. Sanctification reduces liability to error to a minimum, but it does not guarantee infallibility; and while we have an adversary so subtle and a nature so liable to sin, we shall never rise above the need to pray, "Forgive us our trespasses." The vision of the pure heart is always discovering new demands of grace and a new sensibility of sin. It is better to live a sinless life than to say we never sin.

> Jesus, Thou art our King!
> To me Thy succor bring;
> Christ, the mighty One, art Thou,
> Help for all on Thee is laid;
> This the word; I claim it now,
> Send me now the promis'd aid.
>
> High on Thy Father's throne,
> O look with pity down!
> Help, O help, attend my call,
> Captive lead captivity;

King of glory, Lord of all,
Christ, be Lord, be King, to me!

I pant to feel Thy sway,
And only Thee to obey,
Thee my spirit gasps to meet;
This my one, my ceaseless prayer,
Make, O make, my heart Thy seat,
O set up Thy Kingdom there!

Triumph and reign in me,
And spread Thy victory;
Hell, and death, and sin control,
Pride, and wrath, and every foe,
All subdue; through all my soul
Conquering, and to conquer go.

Christian Perfection and Temptation

It is said of Jesus Christ "that he himself hath suffered being tempted,"[1] and also that He "was in all points tempted like as *we are, yet* without sin."[2] The first statement declares the reality of His temptation, and the second certifies its representative character. The Scriptures never speculate upon the nature and character of Christ. No explanation is offered of His temptation, nor of the extent to which He pondered or desired the objects presented to His mind. The facts are stated, and we are able to deduce important conclusions, but though important they are not revealed. Satan was the tempter, so we infer Jesus was open to attack from an evil source. He suffered being tempted, by which we understand there was real conflict in the soul of Christ. The proposals of the tempter appealed to Him. There was a consciousness of something in the forbidden path that was plausible. Otherwise there could be no temptation to sin. He was tempted in "all points like as we are." In all points; not in all forms. There are temptations that come to us that never came to Him, because

---

[1] Hebrews 2:18
[2] Hebrews 4:15

He never experienced many of the relations out of which our temptations spring. For instance, He never was a husband or father, wife or mother. He did not live under twentieth century conditions of life and labor. In these and other respects He had no experience of many temptations with which we are familiar, but in every practical sense He was tempted like as we are. He was tested at every point where temptation can assail, and tried along every avenue by which sin may gain access to the soul.

❧ The Perfect Man Tempted ☙

The temptation of Christ is our warrant for saying that temptation is inseparable from probation. The perfect are subject to assault from Satan and solicitation to evil. Humanity is not dehumanized when the work of grace is perfected in the soul. Some teaching would make Entire Sanctification a process of emasculation. Grace destroys nothing but sin. The "old man" crucified is superseded by the "new man in Christ Jesus." He is still a man. All the appetites remain in the sanctified man. Their order is restored, their direction rectified, and their desires purified. Their gratification is no longer sought in forbidden ways. Every desire is submitted at once to the test of the divine will, and whatever is suspected of being at variance with the standard is at once dismissed. In the sanctified man the desires, the affections, and the will become allies of the conscience. Man may be tempted in another sense than that indicated in James 1:13, 14. The ambiguity which attaches to the English word "temptation" has led to some confusion. Originally it meant just "to try." Hence the noun, attempt, and the adjective, tentative (temptative). It has hardened, however, into a use that indicates trial with an evil purpose. Both uses are found in the Scriptures. In the Old Testament it is more frequently used of righteous than of unrighteous trial; while in the New Testament, prevailingly, but not uniformly, it is used of trying to induce to evil. The first use of the word is in Genesis 22:1: "And it came to pass after these things that God did tempt Abraham." The writer to the Hebrews (11:17) says of the same event, "By faith Abraham, when he was tried." In Psalm 26:2, the psalmist says, "Examine me, O Lord, and prove [try] me; try my reins and my heart." Our Lord is said to have asked a question of Philip to prove him (John 6:6). Writing in the second letter to the Corinthians (13:5), St. Paul exhorts them Saying, "Examine yourselves, whether ye be in the faith; prove your own selves." The words used for "examine" and "prove" could quite rightly be translated "tempt". God tried those at Ephesus who said they were apostles, and found them liars (Rev. 2:2). Jesus was led "of the Spirit into the wilderness to be tempted of the devil" (Matt. 4:1). There is a vital difference between the two uses of the word. It may mean either to solicit or to test. In the first sense Satan tempts men; he entices to evil. In the second sense God proved Abraham. He put him to the proof. Adam was tempted and fell. Jesus was tempted and conquered. In neither was there the lust or proneness due to sinful generation, but both were tempted. Grace cannot make us more perfect than Christ, and if He suffered being tempted we surely shall not escape.

St. James bids us glory in temptation: "My brethren, count it all joy when ye fall into divers temptations; Knowing *this*, that the trying of your faith worketh patience."[3] Again he says, " Blessed *is* the man that endureth temptation: for when he is tried, he shall receive the crown of life, which the Lord hath promised to them that love him."[4]

❧ Sanctification and Temptation ❧

It is a matter of speculation at what point temptation passes beyond the boundary of innocence. Some have argued that, if the temptation advances beyond the intellect and affects the desires, exciting them to action, such desires are always attended with sin. This position cannot be sustained from the Word of God. Desire may be sinful, for Christ Himself has told us that a look may be adultery, and passion, murder; but that is

> *The lust of the flesh may be successfully antagonized and overcome.*

when desire has the consent of the will, and only for prudential or other reasons does not pass into action. What about sinful desire resisted? The lust of the flesh may be successfully antagonized and overcome. Temptation is not sin; it is consent that makes it sin. Entire sanctification purges the nature of its inborn proneness to evil. Dr. W. B. Pope says, "Sanctification in its beginnings, process, and final issues, is the full eradication of the sin itself, which reigning in the unregenerate co-exists with the new life in the regenerate, is

---

[3] James 1:2,3
[4] James 1:12

abolished in the wholly sanctified." Mark the terms! "Reigning in the unregenerate, co-exists with the new life in the regenerate, abolished in the wholly sanctified." It cleanses him of "his own lust" by which he was drawn away and enticed. The desire for gratification by forbidden means is taken away. The soul is cleansed by the cleansing blood of the Son of God. Not only is grace given to resist, the desire to yield is rooted up and cast out of the heart. Sin is loathed because love is perfect.

❧ The Temptations of the Sanctified ❧

This does not mean that sanctification places the soul beyond temptation. On the contrary, it brings it to exceptional exposure. The experience furnishes a new basis of attack. Our Lord's temptation followed His baptism, not only as a matter of time, but of consequence. The temptation was the outcome of the experience. It was upon the testimony of the baptism that the attack was made. If He was "tempted like as we are" it follows that, as we become like Him, we shall be tempted as He was. The wilderness is never far from the Jordan. The relations of the natural and the spiritual have to be adjusted, and Satan will seek to win us back through the demands of the flesh, the problem of bread, and the obligations of common toil. If he fails there, he will test along the avenue of courageous faith, and tempt to presumption and vain glory. The second often succeeds where the first fails. Grace is made the occasion of sin, when we disobey God under cover of faith. The final temptation of Spirit-filled people is to use carnal weapons in spiritual aims. The world is accepted under plea of its service to the kingdom. The peril of these temptations is in their subtlety. To the saints Satan comes as an angel of light. The beast is transformed into the likeness of a lamb. The very elect are deceived, if they cease to live in the Spirit through whom comes discernment as well as power. God is able to keep us from stumbling, and to set us before the presence of His glory without blemish, in exceeding joy, but we need to watch and pray lest we enter into temptation.

Saviour of the sin-sick soul,
Give me faith to make me whole!
Finish Thy great work of grace,
Cut it short in righteousness.

Speak the second time, "Be clean!"
Take away my inbred sin;
Every stumbling-block remove,
Cast it out by perfect love.

Nothing less will I require,
Nothing more can I desire;
None but Christ to me be given!
None but Christ in earth or heaven!

O that I might now decrease!
O that all I am might cease!
Let me into nothing fall,
Let my Lord be all in all!

Christian Perfection: A Second Blessing

There is a deep-rooted prejudice against Christian Perfection as a second definite experience assured to the soul. The prejudice is so great that even convention teachers rarely use the term. Substitutes have been invented which take away the offense because they take off the edge. Both in Regeneration and in Sanctification there is a shrinking from the sharp and definite experience of a crisis. Theology has been taken captive by the modern spirit. The theory of evolution has relegated everything sudden and supernatural to the limbo of superstition. We are impressed by the operations that take millenniums, and suspect whatever is wrought by processes we cannot trace and powers we cannot schedule. We can understand culture, but distrust conversion. Growth appeals to our sense of reason, but a sudden elimination of inherited tendencies is not in harmony with the process of Nature. That is why so much modern preaching is vague and ineffective. It is of the sheet-lightning sort; it shines but does not strike. Glittering generalities may dazzle, but they accomplish nothing. Wesley reproached his preachers in the Launceston Circuit because they "either did not speak of

Perfection at all (the peculiar doctrine committed to our trust) or they speak of it only in general terms, without urging the believers to go on unto Perfection, and to expect it every moment, and wherever this is not done the work of God does not prosper."[1]

❧ Why Call It a Second Blessing? ❧

Is it worthwhile to contend for a term? That depends upon what is involved in its surrender. Not infrequently we hear men told to "call it what they please, it does not matter what you call it if you get it." That is true, and yet the more general terms reveal a dislike of the experience which comes as a crisis. The names substituted are beautifully suggestive and singularly evasive. "A deeper work of Grace," "the Higher Life," and "a Great Blessing" have a gracious and soothing sound, but they lack definiteness, certainty, and assurance.

Experience varies in sanctification as in conversion with temperament and education.

The new names are more indicative of pietism than of testimony. Why this vagueness and laxity in defining Entire Sanctification? True, in matters of life there cannot be the same exactness as in machinery. Experience varies in sanctification as in conversion with temperament and education. No one pleads for uniformity. There are Twelve Gates into the City, and they are equally distributed to all points of the compass. Some enter the blessing as they enter the Kingdom without consciousness of time or place, but an

---

[1] John Wesley's Journals, August 14, 1776. (parenthetical in original)

assurance is given them of cleansing as of pardon and reconciliation. Whether we call it a Second Blessing or not, that is what it is. It is distinct from Regeneration and subsequent to it. Those who contend that they received all that is involved in salvation when they were "born again" do not distinguish between potentiality and conscious possession. The man is in the child, but manhood can be attained only in stages.

The experience is the crisis when the immaturity of "Babes in Christ" passes into the mature consciousness of the full-grown. In pagan religions there is a period of initiation. It is said that the process is associated with things that are vile, but the vital point is that it marks a crisis, a transition, an introduction to the powers and responsibilities of manhood. The reproach of the Corinthian Christians was that they had passed the age of adolescence and were still children in experience and understanding. They failed to understand because they had missed the experience of initiation. The "First" Blessing comprehends justification, regeneration, and adoption; and the "Second" Blessing brings cleansing of the carnal mind, and the anointing of the Holy Spirit. The term is not scriptural, but that is true of many doctrinal terms, and there can be no objection so long as it stands for an equivalent of biblical teaching.

❧ The Second Blessing a Weslyan Doctrine ❧

All teaching of holiness as a definite experience agrees that it is for the "elect through grace." It is for those who are born again of the Spirit, for Christians and not for unbelievers. That is by faith, of grace, and by the Spirit. Like conversion it involves a crisis, an acceptance, and a confession. Wesley taught it as a definite blessing instantaneously received by faith. He held that believers are not entirely sanctified in regeneration, but are delivered from the remains of sin by a second work of grace. He called it a "second blessing" and a "second change." He tested those who professed the experience with the care and fidelity of a scientist. He cross-examined the witnesses with the severity of a lawyer. His conclusions were not based upon a few exceptional cases, and so sure was he of the doctrine, that he says if he is mistaken in this he is clearly convinced his whole meaning of Scripture must be mistaken. So strongly convinced was he that three months before his death he wrote:

"If we can prove that any of our local preachers or leaders, either directly or indirectly, speak against it, let him be a local preacher or leader no longer."[2]

With some, Dr. W. B. Pope has more weight than John Wesley. In his sermon on the Healing of the Blind Man, in Mark 8, he says:

"I have sometimes very delicately scrupled at this, that, and the other expression, and I have wondered whether it is right to speak of a 'second blessing' ... in the face of this text, and in the face of the experience of multitudes of our fathers; in the face of multitudes now living, and in the face of the deep instinct, the hope and desire of my own unworthy heart, I will never again write or speak against the phraseology

---

[2] From a letter addressed to Adam Clarke, November 26, 1790.

referred to."

I heard these words from his own lips, and shall never forget the humility and emotion with which they were spoken. He lacked the assertive confidence of shallower men, but his testimony was not wanting, and his spirit was its daily exposition. There has been much confusion and many abuses of the doctrine, but thousands can testify to the experience.

It is difficult to choose, for there is "a great cloud of witnesses," and there is not space to tell all their testimony; but let Charles Inwood, a world-known Keswick speaker and missioner, give his. He was a Weslyan, and reared in the best type of Weslyan home. While still a boy at school he was converted, knew it, and lived it. Then when he had become a minister there came to him a wonderful experience of Sanctification - a distinctly second work of grace. There had been no backsliding, no Blackness, no compromise, but there came to him a great soul-hunger, a need of cleansing, and a longing to be filled with the Spirit of God. This is how it came.

"God led me on Friday morning, simply as a little child, to trust Him for this priceless gift, the fullness of the Holy Spirit. By simple, naked faith I took the gift, but I was not conscious of receiving anything. All through that day there seemed even a deeper dryness and dullness in one's soul - no new pulsations, no new sense of the presence of God... Sunday morning just as dry as ever; and the Sunday morning service came, and during the proclamation of the message, there came silently stealing into my heart a strange new sense of ease and rest and peace. That is how it began; and then it deepened, hour by hour during the day, deepened in the service in the evening, and in the after-meeting it seemed to culminate in one great tidal wave of the glory of God that swelled and submerged and interpenetrated, and broke me down in silent, holy adoration in God's presence."

Out of that baptism there emerged the Apostolic ministry of the sanctified Charles Inwood, and its rivers flowed to the ends of the earth.

The doctrine is scriptural, and that is more important than being Weslyan, but with the Weslyan there rests a heavier responsibility than most. It was for this testimony the Weslyan Church was raised up, and this is the special "depositum" committed to its trust.

> Ever fainting with desire,
> For Thee, O Christ, I call;
> Thee I restlessly require,
> I want my God, my all!
> Jesus, dear redeeming Lord,
> I wait Thy coming from above;
> Help me, Saviour, speak the word,
> And perfect me in love.
>
> Lord, if I on Thee believe,
> The second gift impart;
> With the indwelling spirit give
> A new, a contrite heart;
> If with love Thy heart is stored,
> If now o'er me Thy mercies move,
> Help me, Saviour, speak the word,

And perfect me in love.

Let me gain my calling's hope,
O make the sinner clean!
Dry corruption's fountain up,
Cut off the entail of sin;
Take me into Thee, my Lord,
And I shall then no longer rove;
Help me, Saviour, speak the word,
And perfect me in love.

Grant me now the bliss to feel
Of those that are in Thee;
Son of God, Thyself reveal,
Engrave Thy name on me;
As in heaven be here adored,
And let me now the promise prove;
Help me, Saviour, speak the word,
And perfect me in love.

Do the Scriptures Teach a Second Blessing?

It is easier to prove the doctrine of a Second Blessing from John Wesley, than from the Bible. The demand for scriptural proof calls a halt. In creeds and theologies, truth is defined and stated clearly and dogmatically. They give the results of analysis and classification, without hint of the processes by which the conclusions were reached. From ecclesiastical declarations and theological definitions, it is easy to prove the need for a second work of grace in believers. The Bible, however, is not so explicit. Its doctrines are neither stated in dogmatic utterances nor expressed in syllogisms. There is much theology that is not biblical, and most people prefer to have their doctrines formulated for them. The task of seeking truth at first hand is not easy. Christian truth has been evolved through long and varied processes. It is embodied -- not to say embedded -- in a series of books in which the unity does not appear upon the surface. The raw material has to be analyzed and systematized. Nothing must be imported, nothing suppressed, nothing "squared." The doctrine must be comprehensive enough to include all the Scriptures have to contribute. There must be space for apparently contradictory propositions. No statement may override another. Proof by isolated texts can be made to prove anything. Truth flows through a thousand channels, and doctrine must gather up all phases in its ultimate statement. For this reason it is not enough to buttress a statement by texts; the statement must be the final issue of all the texts. The proof is an accumulation of truth. Conviction is not begotten of logic. A man does not believe a doctrine because something proves it; he believes it because everything proves it. That is why the things of which we are surest are always most difficult to prove. The Second Blessing is not in a text; it is in the whole Bible. Because the man who has found it sees it everywhere, it is difficult for him to prove it anywhere. The multiplicity of proof bewilders in the presence of one who cannot see, but the experience itself brings the supreme Teacher. There is an unction of the Holy One by which the sanctified are led into the Truth. The pure in heart see. Love made perfect sanctifies all life, and perfects the knowledge of divine things. Hereby we know, and know that we know, if we keep His commandments.

❧ Hidden Treasures ❧

People often ask why a doctrine so important is not more explicitly stated and commanded in the Bible. The same question applies to all doctrine within the Kingdom. The command to repent and believe, the necessity of forgiveness and regeneration, are definite and explicit enough, because these are concerned with them that are without. When once the boundary is passed, truth has to be discovered. It cannot be mechanically or magically poured into a man. Spiritual things are spiritually discerned. They cannot be passed on as articles of faith. Every soul has to find them for itself. Jesus commanded His disciples to tell no man He was the Christ. He Himself had many things to say, but His lips were sealed. The Spirit leads each into the possession of truth that can only be received by the experiment of personal faith. To those who have entered in, there is given a glorious assurance and much treasure which they cannot divide with those who have it not. All they can say is: This is our testimony -- go and "buy for yourselves."

Those who are keen to know that they may possess will find it fully set forth in the Scriptures. There is no other guide, nor any other authority. The Bible is its own interpreter, and they that will to know that they may

> *Those who have entered the experience see the teaching from Genesis to Revelation.*

do, will not seek in vain. It is an experience that must be rooted and grounded in the Word of God.

It must be admitted that passages urged as the basis of a Second Blessing carry little weight, apart from those who have the key to them in their own hearts. There are smiles of incredulity, mingled with pity, when the blessing is discovered in Exodus and Leviticus; in the architecture, furniture, and ordinances of the tabernacle; as well as in distinctions of speech that seem forced and fanciful. So marked has this become that the method of interpretation is labeled and tabooed. But those who have entered the experience see the teaching from Genesis to Revelation, and the method has the warrant of apostolic example.

❧ The Scriptural Basis ❧

That the Scriptures require us to be holy, no one denies. Without holiness no man can ever enter heaven. Neither is it denied that provision is made in Christ for our sanctification. He came to save from sin. That involves more than pardon and deliverance from its dominion. Sin is of the heart, and its presence is more offensive than its acts of transgression. Christ redeems, that He may cleanse and restore. Possibility of sin remains in the regenerate. It does not reign, but it remains. Of that there can be no doubt. Scripture and experience affirm it. The Christians at Corinth were regenerated, and yet were acting carnal (1 Cor. 1:2; 3:1-3). They were exhorted to cleanse themselves "from all filthiness of the flesh and spirit, perfecting holiness in the fear of God" (2 Cor. 7:1). The Galatians had received the spirit of adoption, and to them the Apostle said, "The flesh lusteth against the Spirit, and the Spirit against the flesh" (Gal. 5:17). Thus people already in a state of grace are urged to an experience of cleansing and fullness. Count Zinzendorf's teaching, that "all true believers are not only saved from the dominion of sin, but from the being of inward as well as outward sin, so that it no longer remains in them," is utterly without warrant. The New Testament saints were true believers, and the possibility of carnality remained in them. That there is cleansing from the being of inward sin, is abundantly manifest from God's Word. The commands assume it, and the promises declare it. "The blood of Jesus His Son cleanseth us from all sin."[1] That cleansing is by faith. There is no other condition, but faith is impossible without conviction. It is a definite act with a definite aim. If the soul is to be cleansed from sin, it must take place somewhere between regeneration and heaven; and that point is reached where faith claims the blessing. The Apostle desired to come again to the believers at Thessalonica that he might "perfect that which was lacking in their faith,"[2] and the desire was expressed in the prayer:

"And the very God of peace sanctify you wholly; and *I pray God* your whole spirit and soul and body be preserved blameless unto the coming of our Lord Jesus Christ. Faithful is He that calleth you, who will also do it."[3]

> I ask the gift of righteousness,
> The sin-subduing power,
> Power to believe, and go in peace,
> And never grieve Thee more.
>
> I ask the blood-bought pardon sealed,
> The liberty from sin,
> The grace infused, the love revealed,
> The Kingdom fixed within.
>
> Thou hear'st me for salvation pray,
> Thou seest my heart's desire;

---

[1] 1 John 1:7
[2] 1 Thessalonians 3:10
[3] 1 Thessalonians 5:23, 24

The Call to Christian Perfection

Made ready in Thy powerful day,
Thy fullness I require.

My vehement soul cries out opprest,
Impatient to be freed;
Nor can I, Lord, nor will I rest,
Till I am saved indeed.

Art Thou not able to convert?
Art Thou not willing, too?
To change this old, rebellious heart,
To conquer and renew?

Thou canst, Thou wilt, I dare believe,
So arm me with Thy power,
That I to sin shall never cleave,
Shall never feel it more.

Is Christian Perfection Attainable?

Whether Christian Perfection is attainable in this life is a question of first importance. There is a perfection that is not. The final perfecting of grace awaits its consummation in glory. This is the perfection to which St. Paul said he had not yet attained, but to which he was ever pressing forward as the great end for which he was apprehended in Christ Jesus. That is the perfection of finality, whereas Christian Perfection is one of adjustment and completeness. It does not even imply maturity, much less finality. Christian Perfection is neither physical nor mental. It is in the heart, the motive, and the will. Can the love of God be perfected in the soul in this life? God commands it and expects it. The experience is described by a variety of terms, but they all represent the same truth from different aspects. Wesley spoke of it as Entire Sanctification; a term which is scriptural and intelligible. No honest believer in the Bible can deny the necessity for sanctification. Without it no man can see the Lord. Therefore, it must be attainable before the manifestation of God to the soul. There is nothing in the death of the body that can perfect the work of sanctification in the soul, and the Scriptures give no hope of purgatorial perfecting. If Christian Perfection is attainable at all it must be in the conditions of our present life.

❧ Objections to Perfection ❧

There are those, however, who do not believe it possible in our mortal state. Some objections are the result of confusion. For instance, it is argued that Christian Perfection involves finality. No heresy based upon the corruption of God's Word dies harder than this! It is amazing that Bible teachers should say that this state would "admit of no progression," that if it were attained the Christian's "work would be finished and his obligations discharged"; that there would be no more warfare, "nor further need of prayer or the means of grace." Such teaching in some vague way regards the body as inherently antagonistic to God, and irreclaimably corrupt. It confounds moral corruption with physical limitation. The sinless life of Christ is the absolute denial of any such doctrine. The life of God has to be realized, appropriated and exemplified by those who are still in the flesh. Death has no saving efficacy. Not a single passage of scripture can be found that associates the cleansing of the soul with physical dissolution.

> *Not a single passage of scripture can be found that associates the cleansing of the soul with physical dissolution.*

There is a theory which regards Christian Perfection as "metaphysically attainable," and denies the fact of actual attainment. It is too subtle and too devout to bluntly deny the doctrine, but it regards it as an imputed perfection and not an actual possession. In this teaching inbred sin is not eradicated but repressed, and holiness is not imparted but imputed. Here is a summary of this doctrine:

"He who is our Great High Priest before God is pure, without sin. God sees Him as such, and He stands for us who are His people, and we are accepted in Him. His holiness is ours by imputation. Standing in Him we are in the sight of God, holy as He is holy, and pure as Christ is pure. God looks at our Representative, and He sees us in Him. We are complete in Him who is our spotless and glorious Head."

Such a theory makes void the law through faith. It is a process of sheer make-believe, by which God shuts His eyes to our real state and agrees to accept a fiction for a fact. It makes man holy by exemption, instead of by righteousness. Such teaching contravenes the plainest statements of God's Word in which Christ is declared to have made provision for man's deliverance from all sin. Christ died not that He might secure our exemption from the law, but "that the righteousness of the law might be fulfilled in us, who walk not after the flesh but after the Spirit."[1]

❧ Has It Been Attained? ☙

Next to the authority of the Scriptures is the testimony of them that believe. The question of fact as to the reality of this experience can be settled by testimony alone. Whether a man loves God with all his heart is known only to himself and his God. No man can search the heart of another.

---

[1] Romans 8:4

The only test we have is in such terms of scripture as: "Whoso keepeth his word, in him verily is the love of God perfected,"[2] and "he that saith he abideth in him ought himself also so to walk even as he walked."[3] Ought surely implies possibility; and it is a sufficient test without inventing others. All hypothetical tests tend to morbid introspection or self-complacent Pharisaism. Apart from all fads, cranks, and absurdities, so often associated with the profession of this state of grace, we have to ask whether it has ever been a conscious reality in the soul of a believer. It is not a question whether some may not have been mistaken, but whether all are mistaken. The question cannot be settled by quoting the number of those who were leaders in the Church and conscious that they did not love God with all their heart. The deepest piety is not generally found among the leaders of the Church. The witness of one man whose eyes have been opened is of greater weight than the opinions of all the leaders of religious thought.

❧ An Assured Possession ❧

Thousands whose integrity was beyond reproach have testified to its possession. They were in a glorious succession. John Wesley bore a similar testimony, and thousands of his people professed a like experience. Wesley sifted their evidence. He found them sane, sincere, and saintly. Their intelligence was clear, and their logic sound. The facts could be

---

[2] 1 John 2:5
[3] 1 John 2:6

verified, and the fruits were manifest. Either their witness must be received, or there is an end of credible testimony. The experience was based upon Scripture. It came through the promises, and proved them to be Yea and Amen. They were sanctified in truth, and the truth was demonstrated in their sanctification. In a moment by appropriating faith they became conscious of heart purity and indwelling fullness of the divine Presence. The experience was assured to them by the witness of the Spirit.

It has been the chief glory of Weslyanism to proclaim this experience as the duty and privilege of all. Those who entered into the blessing were urged to bear definite witness to the experience, and to abide in fellowship with those who had received, or were seeking after this grace. The type of piety it produced became as distinctive as the witness. I would like to quote what Wesley says of Jane Cooper in his preface to her Letters:

"All here is strong sterling sense, strictly agreeable to sound reason. Here are no extravagant flights, no mystic reveries, no unscriptural enthusiasm. The sentiments are all just and noble; the result of a fine natural understanding cultivated by conversation, thinking, reading, and true Christian experience. At the same time they show a heart as well improved as the understanding; truly devoted to God, and filled in a very uncommon degree with the entire fruit of His Spirit. . . . This strong, genuine sense is expressed in such style as none would expect from a young servant maid; a style not only simple and artless in the highest degree but likewise clear, lively, proper: every phrase, every word being so well chosen, yea, and so well placed, that it is not easy to mend it. And such an inexpressible sweetness runs through the whole as art would in vain strive to imitate."

It would be difficult to find a more perfect delineation of the spiritual experience and character of a Weslyan. You will observe that Jenny Cooper was a servant-maid. The Weslyans insisted that this grace is without respect of persons, and that it does not depend upon natural endowments, intellectual culture, or on favorable opportunities. It is not a cult. The experience is neither purely intellectual nor purely emotional, but a mingling of sound understanding and deep feeling.

Sometimes in a rapture of unspeakable joy and at other times with a deep sense of humility and peace, men have realized that God sanctified their hearts by faith. Life was raised to a new plane of experience and power. Death was swallowed up in life more abundant. Defeat ended in the victory of overcoming power. Fellowship entered into more intimate communion and a larger inheritance. They lived with a new sense of the divine Presence, and served in the strength of the indwelling Spirit. It is attainable, for it has been attained.

> O might I this moment cease
> From every work of mine,
> Find the perfect holiness,
> The righteousness divine!
> Let me Thy salvation see;
> Let me do Thy perfect will;
> Live in glorious liberty,
> And all Thy fullness feel.

Is Christian Perfection Attainable?

O cut short the work, and make
Me now a creature new!
For Thy truth and mercy's sake
The gracious wonder show;
Call me forth Thy witness, Lord,
Let my life declare Thy power;
To Thy perfect love restored,
O let me sin no more!

Fain would I the truth proclaim
That makes me free indeed,
Glorify my Saviour's name,
And all its virtues spread;
Jesus all our wants relieves,
Jesus, mighty to redeem,
Saves, and to the utmost saves,
All those that come to Him.

The Negations of Christian Perfection

One of the most common criticisms of Holiness is that it is a religion of negation, inhibition, and prohibition. These are not my words, and I have taken the trouble to look them up in the dictionary. The sense in which negation is used means the absence of certain qualities in anything. Inhibition is to restrain, to hold in, or keep back. Prohibition is to forbid, and implies the command of a superior authority. Taken together as a criticism, they complain that a life of holiness is made up chiefly of negatives, that it is a life of repression, and a series of things not to be done. The criticism is the opposite of the truth. It is not negative but positive, not restraint but freedom, not mechanism but life. Can anything be more positive than Love made Perfect? Can anything be more gloriously free than the liberty of an emancipated soul? Can anything be so free from the bondage of external authority or the mechanism of tyrannical rules as Life in the Spirit? Full Salvation fills up that which is lacking, gives fullness and spontaneity to all the resources of vitality and power, and lifts life above the legalism of systems and ordinances of the flesh. Salvation is full, present, and free.

♪ Negations Not Negative ♪

I hesitated between the words negation and negative, but there is a difference between an absence and a denial. Light is the negation of darkness, but it does not deny its existence; and it is in this way that the perfect is described by the opposites which are not there. It is a familiar way of describing perfection in the Scriptures. The perfection of the Spirit-filled ministry of Jesus is described in terms of qualities that were strikingly absent. "I will put my spirit upon him. . . . He shall not strive, nor cry; neither shall any man hear his voice in the streets. A bruised reed shall he not break, and smoking flax shall he not quench".[1] These characteristics are absent, because of the perfection of the opposites. The defects are excluded, because of the majestic perfection of His truth, humility, faith, and love. In the same way the Apostle James argues the perfection of the whole man from the absence of offense in speech: "If any man offend not in word, the same *is* a perfect man"[2]. The glory of heaven is described in the same way. "They shall hunger no more, neither thirst any more; neither shall the sun light on them, nor any heat . . . and God shall wipe away all tears from their eyes."[3] No hunger; no thirst; no weariness; no tears! In the heavenly land there will be no curse, no night, no candle, no sun, no moon, and no temple. The perfection of glory is revealed by their absence. They are excluded, because they are incompatible. So it is in

---

[1] Matthew 12:18-20
[2] James 3:2
[3] Revelation 7:16, 17

the Spirit-filled life. The negations, inhibitions, and prohibitions are not labels or bandages; they are incompatibles. St. Paul uses the five strongest words he can find, to set forth the incongruity of alliance and compromise with the world, the flesh, and the devil. What fellowship? What communion? What concord? What part? What agreement? "Wherefore come out from among them, and be ye separate, saith the Lord" (2 Cor. 6:14-17). The perfection is known by the things not there.

❧ No Fear ❧

Full salvation saves from fear. It is amazing how the Lord seeks to save from fear. In the Old Testament and in the New He rebukes our fears, calls to courage, and promises peace. "Fear not, for I am with Thee." Zacharias proclaimed in the coming of the Messiah a gospel of holiness and righteousness, in which service should be without fear.

"That he would grant unto us, that we being delivered out of the hand of our enemies might serve him without fear, In holiness and righteousness before him, all the days of our life"[4]. The enemies in the mind of Zacharias may have been the Romans, but he was a priest, and it was of other enemies he thought in the mission of the Messiah, or he would not have given such prominence to the holiness and righteousness to be lived before Him. Holiness is rightness of character, righteousness is the rightness of conduct. Before Him! Life is to be in His presence, acceptable to Him in thought, disposition, and desire, and approved in conduct, judgment,

---

[4] Luke 1:74, 75

and speech. Without fear, because without condemnation.

"There is no fear in love" (1 John 4:18). Perfect love casteth out fear, and our love is made perfect in the indwelling of the God of love by the gift of His Spirit. No fear means the fullness of love and the perfection of trust. That is one of the negations of Love made perfect. Holiness is a life in which there is no fear. No fear! None whatever, of any kind, or any place? That is what no fear means. "I will fear no evil." I will trust in Him at all times. I will trust and not be afraid. If God be for us, with us, and in us, of whom and of what shall we be afraid? He undertakes supplies. He chooses our way, and guides our feet. He fights our battles, and makes us more than conquerors. He knows all things -- all about our needs, all about our temper and temperament, all about our lot, all about life, and all about death. He fills the heart with love, and asks implicitly for the trust in which there is no fear.

❧ No Care ❧

What a care-burdened world this is! Jesus summed up its need in the burden of unrest, and promised a heart free from care. The supreme gift of God in Christ is peace. He is the God of Peace, and the gift of Jesus is the peace of God. He not only gives the divine peace, but He keeps in perfect peace. What is perfect peace but peace without anxiety and without care? "Be anxious for nothing." That is the command and promise of Jesus. The fully saved live without care. Just inside my study door is the word "Ataraxia" in letters of gold. It was the gift of a friend years ago after a sermon I had preached on the word. Nearly every stranger that comes asks what it means, and when I answer "Without care," they pause and say, "Ah, is it possible?" Yes, wherever the Spirit of God dwells in the heart, sanctifying, perfecting, filling, unto all the will of God. Business people sometimes hint that I should find it different if I were in business, but there are business men who have found the life that is radiant and without care. Often I am told that I should find it different if in these days I had sons and daughters, and that, I can imagine, would be quite

> *The children of God have no more right to worry, than they have to get drunk.*

likely; but they would be His as well as mine, and I cannot believe He would fail me. He never has failed. He cares, that I may be free from care. The children of God have no more right to worry, than they have to get drunk. In the Spirit-sanctified, Spirit-possessed, Spirit-strengthened, Spirit-perfected, there is no anxiety, no worry, no care. Blessed negation! Blessed inhibition! I ask no greater blessedness than the perfection supplied by such blessed absences.

❧ No Blame ❧

NO BLAME. There are people who imagine that a life of full salvation pretends to be beyond need or capability of progress or improvement. It is really difficult to be patient with such stupidity, especially in those who are the accredited teachers and leaders of the Church. Christian Perfection is defined by its adjective. It is neither final nor flawless. It is a definite work of grace, by which the nature is cleansed of its bias to evil and is made to be partaker of the Divine nature. Every part is sanctified and made conformable to the Divine will. It does not make mistakes impossible or discipline unnecessary, but it does answer the prayer of the Apostle in 1 Thessalonians 5:23, 24: "And the very God of peace sanctify you wholly; and *I pray God* your whole spirit and soul and body be preserved blameless unto the coming of our Lord Jesus Christ. Faithful *is* he that calleth you, who also will do *it*."

Ye ransom'd sinners, hear,
The prisoners of the Lord,
And wait till Christ appear,
According to His word;
Rejoice in hope, rejoice with me,
We shall from all our sins be free.

In God we put our trust;
If we our sins confess,
Faithful He is, and just,
From all unrighteousness
To cleanse us all, both you and me;
We shall from all our sins be free.

Surely in us the hope
Of glory shall appear;
Sinners, your heads lift up,
And see redemption near;
Again I say, rejoice with me,
We shall from all our sins be free.

The word of God is sure,
And never can remove,
We shall in heart be pure,
And perfected in love;
Rejoice in hope, rejoice with me,
We shall from all our sins be free.

Difficulties About Christian Perfection

Among the many letters received on the above subject, here is one that expresses in a typical way the difficulties of many devout and earnest Christian people:

"I have been much interested and more than intrigued by your article, 'The Spirit of Holiness.' It has moved me to a deeper yearning for holiness.

"I am one of those people you speak of, whose mistake it is to suppose that holiness comes by a gradual growth in grace, and I quite agree, from my inner experience, that 'its mischief is that it never gets there.' One is always hungering and thirsting, but just as surely, one is always conscious of deep defilement of nature which constantly prevents anything approaching the 'heart made perfect.' If I could realize that this perfection is really as you say, not a thing to be attained, but a gift of grace in the Holy Ghost, how gladly would I claim it!

"Yet, to be quite candid, I feel that the consciousness of a heart made free from all inner sinfulness, would soon lose its humility, and perhaps lose its sympathy with sinful people. I have in mind one Christian worker who claimed the blessing of holiness some years ago, and is never tired of telling how she has been kept without sin for this period. But her testimony never moves me, as does the cry of some heart yearning after more of God, and if one must be quite honest, this good woman is rather avoided.

"I can quite understand, regarding the positive side of holiness, that health never hinders growth; but to have health means to be free from disease, free from sin. Would you be so good as to explain to my dense mind the difference between the freedom from sin which you term 'Perfection,' and which you term 'Finality,' for I fear I am partly guilty of this 'most common and senseless confusion.' I know I am almost hopelessly ignorant, but, believe me, I really desire to know, if it be possible, to be made perfect. So if you should feel that you can make it the matter of some future article - this difference between perfection of grace and perfection of glory - maybe it would vastly help other ignorant and struggling sinners like myself."

❧ The Confession ❧

Perhaps it will be best to begin with the confession. For years my correspondent has supposed that holiness comes by a gradual growth in grace, but testifies from experience "that it never gets there." That is the experience of everybody who hopes to grow into the blessing. It never comes by growth, either unurged or forced. The evil grows with the good until the evil is purged out. Surely it cannot be consistent with the gospel of a Saviour who is able to save to the uttermost, that we should be for ever striving and for ever failing! His purpose is that we should be saved with a present, free, and full salvation, and His grace is equal to His purpose. Salvation is not of works, but of grace through faith. The work is not begun in grace and perfected in works. It is the gift of God.

I am quite aware of the fascination of evolution in spiritual life. Professor Drummond's <u>Natural Law in the Spiritual World</u> captures by its charm rather than convinces by its logic. The theory of evolution breaks down, both in Nature and in Grace. There are creative epochs which lift life into a new plane, implant a new quality, and impart a new power. The experience of the perfecting of grace is a crisis and an epoch. Tens of thousands have testified to the experience, and not one of them ever achieved it by endeavor. Without exception, they received it as a gift of grace through faith.

✌ The Objection ☙

A definite objection is raised. It is a strange comment on the growth and the hungering and thirsting of the soul, to be told that a perfect salvation is neither believed in nor desired. There is a fear lest "the consciousness of a heart made free from all inner sinfulness would lose its humility." That is rather confused logic. How can salvation from the disposition to pride lead to the loss of humility? Is it the sense of sin that makes us humble? If so, how was our sinless Lord meek and lowly in heart? It is not the presence of sin that makes the heart lowly. On such a basis of reckoning, the more sin would yield the greater humility. The blood that cleanses from all sin

> *A heart of compassion is the fruit of holiness.*

purges out of the heart all pride. Lowliness and meekness come of the vision by which the pure in heart see God. The blessing of full salvation saves from pride and envy and all false estimates of worth and virtue. It is stranger still, to imagine that holiness makes us hard and unsympathetic toward sinful people. A heart of compassion is the fruit of holiness. The yearning pity of Romans 9 has its springs in the experience of the eighth chapter. The sinful cannot love sinners unto salvation. The unsatisfied has nothing to give to those who perish of hunger. Holiness brings the soul into fellowship with the redeeming Son of God. When believers rejoice in its possession, sinners are awakened and saved. John Wesley has left it on record as his deliberate judgment that, "when Christian Perfection is not strongly and explicitly preached, there is seldom any remarkable blessing from God; and consequently little addition to the Society, and little life in the members of it."[1] My friend should read some Weslyan biographies, and see how the experience of holiness brought to the heart a consuming passion for souls.

❧ The Terrible Example ❧

We are all familiar with the ghastly caricatures of the doctrine, and it is hardly worthy of an enlightened believer to judge an experience by its failures. It has its true witnesses, and it is by them it must be judged. Spirituality has its perils, and our Lord warned us against censoriousness and hypocrisy.

---

[1] From a letter addressed to George Merryweather, February 8, 1766

Every doctrine has its cranks who regard something important as all-important, but ignorance should not be confused with intention, and it is for those who know better to judge discreetly and set a better example. Counterfeits argue actual genuineness, and it is for us to find the true. Holiness does not make people repellent, but radiant. They are the people of the singing heart and the shining face.

✍ The Difficulty ✍

The real difficulty seems to be in the term "perfection." I have been explaining it for thirty years, and failure to understand the use of the term in two different senses is amazing. Take Philippians 3. The apostle disavows perfection in verse 12, and affirms it in verse 15. The two cannot mean the same in such contradictory statements. The first obviously refers to a future perfecting in the glory of the resurrection; the other is a present experience. In the present he is perfect, but not perfected. There is no finality in the perfection of grace, but in the resurrection grace will be perfected in the consummation of redemption. The great prayer for perfection in Hebrews 13:20,21[2], is the best statement of both the doctrine and the experience. It is being made perfect in every good thing to do His will, and if grace cannot do this it is useless to talk of an uttermost salvation.

---

[2] Now the God of peace, that brought again from the dead our Lord Jesus, that great shepherd of the sheep, through the blood of the everlasting covenant, Make you perfect in every good work to do his will, working in you that which is wellpleasing in his sight, through Jesus Christ; to whom *be* glory for ever and ever. Amen

The Call to Christian Perfection

Now, e'en now, I yield, I yield,
With all my sins to part;
Jesus, speak my pardon sealed,
And purify my heart;
Purge the love of sin away,
Then I into nothing fall;
Then I see the perfect day,
And Christ is all in all.

Jesus, now our hearts inspire
With that pure love of Thine;
Kindle now the heavenly fire,
To brighten and refine;
Purify our faith like gold,
All the dross of sin remove;
Melt our spirits down, and mold
Into Thy perfect love.

The Prayer for Christian Perfection

"Now the God of peace, that brought again from the dead our Lord Jesus, that great shepherd of the sheep, through the blood of the everlasting covenant, Make you perfect in every good work to do his will, working in you that which is wellpleasing in his sight, through Jesus Christ; to whom *be* glory for ever and ever. Amen."[1]

To that prayer I say Amen, and to that covenant I set my seal.

It is not for any man to say he is perfect. The doctrine is scriptural and the defense of it is sound, but the profession of the experience in terms of perfection is not to be commended. It may be true, but it is not expedient. Testimony should never need to be explained. If a man were to say he was perfect, he would need always to safeguard his testimony by explaining what he did not mean. Even then most people would remember the statement and forget the qualifications. It is well to leave the witness to our perfection to other people, and yet the experience cannot be retained without confession. It is assured to the soul by the witness of the Holy Spirit, and what He witnesses we have also to testify. The word may be

---

[1] Hebrews 13:20-21

inexpedient, but the reality must not be refused because the label is not acceptable. It is the experience that matters. Other terms have been used, but they are less expressive than those of scripture. Perfect love is scriptural and interpretative. Sanctification is also a scriptural word, but less popular in this country than in America. Full salvation is comprehensive and less definite, and that is true also of the terms which set forth the fullness of the Spirit. "Christian Perfection" would still be best if we talked Greek, but we speak English and to English-speaking people who have no means of distinguishing between the perfection of grace for efficiency in all the will of God, and the perfection of grace in the consummation of glory, between fitness and finality.

❧ Praying For Perfection ❧

Perfection belongs to the language of prayer. Christian truth finds sublimest expression in prayer. There are no expositions of faith like those in the inspired prayer of Holy Scripture. Language finds its wings in the prayer-life of the soul. Prayer is an exercise that calls for every faculty of man's nature. We have all known people who were naturally slow of speech who were wonderfully gifted in prayer. One reason may be that we talk more freely to God than to anyone else. I remember presiding over a Conference to which there was submitted a resolution on the union of the churches. There was a phrase in it I did not quite like, and I asked that it might be withdrawn. The mover of the resolution expressed surprise that I should make such a request, for the words were quoted from my own prayer at the previous Sunday morning service. There was a laugh at the expense of the president, until I assured them that I said many things to God that I never said to anyone else. Hannah poured out her soul in prayer to God. That is prayer, and in such prayer there are no boundaries or restraints. God knows what we mean. There is no need to weigh our thoughts or measure our words,

Nowhere are we so conscious that we are not perfect as in His presence.

lest the dictionary should condemn us. We pour them all out knowing that God looks at the heart, and nowhere are we so conscious that we are not perfect as in His presence. We know that above all things we seek to do His will, and our hearts are assured before Him, but our holy things need His grace and the cleansing of His blood. Prayer reviews life and motive in the light of His countenance. There is always something to correct, something to improve, something to claim. Prayer cannot ask too much. Hope dwells within the veil. Faith goes in to possess. We pray not only that we may be perfect in every good thing to do His will, but that we may be perfected in the consummation of grace in the glory of our glorious Lord. In prayer faith finds its function and its creed. Therefore, pray!

❧ Perfect In Every Good Thing To Do His Will ❧

Prayer is definitely concerned with the will of God. To do His will we must know what it is, have grace to will it, and to do it. Both are found in prayer. The Perfection is the perfecting of every good thing. The evil things have been done away. It is the good that needs to be perfected. The prayer includes every good thing. In many there remains some good not perfected. When Brother Brice preached in the College Chapel he took the Potter for his subject, and told us some things the commentators did not know. He told us that the vessel on the wheel was not spoiled by some foreign element like stone or glass, wood or iron, but by something of the same nature as itself. It was a bit of clay, and it was quite as good as the rest, but it had not been tempered to the proper pliability. It was not made perfect for its purpose. All the rest was all right, but it was all spoiled because that bit of good clay had not been made perfect for the will of the potter. That illustration tells its own story. The trouble is the imperfect good thing.

Christian Perfection is surrender to, acceptance of, and efficiency in, all the will of God. It is not the attainment of some mystical ecstasy, or the achievement of some heroic sacrifice, but just doing the will of God out of a pure heart. Some people invent tests for themselves that God never imposed. One man I knew was kept from the joy of unreserved surrender for years because he was afraid God would send him to China. God never wanted him for China. Neurotic piety is always inventing impossible heroics. It keeps good people on the jump from one impossibility to another.

❧ The Guaranty To Faith ❧

God has given guaranties of His ability and good

faith. It is not a question of man's will and ability, but of God's purpose and power. I believe in holiness, because I believe in the holiness of God. I am not able, but He is able. Unbelief measures God by man. Faith measures man by God. Unbelief asks if God can. Faith affirms His ability to do. Can God? God can. His very nature demands it, for He is the God of Peace. He makes peace. He gives peace; even perfect peace. There are no antagonisms He cannot reconcile, no dislocations He cannot adjust, no discords He cannot harmonize, no faults He cannot remedy, no diseases He cannot heal, no lack He cannot supply. He is the God of peace, and peace is the perfect relation of every part to every other part, and of all the parts to the whole.

He has proved His power. He brought again from the dead our Lord Jesus. The resurrection of our Lord from the dead is not mentioned elsewhere in the Epistle to the Hebrews, and it is cited here as a guaranty of God's power to make His people perfect. The resurrection of our Lord Jesus is the New Testament standard of measurement for the power of God. It is the big thing by which all other things are measured. In the Old Testament it was the Red Sea. In the New Testament it is the empty grave. This is the example of what God can do. If He did that, He can do this. He is able, I believe.

He has provided a Great Saviour. The Risen Lord is the "Great Shepherd." He called Himself the Good Shepherd. God calls Him the Great Shepherd. After all salvation is not a question of mechanism, but a personal relationship. The Shepherd is everything to His flock. He protects and provides, leads and loves, heals and helps, corrects and controls. The

Lamb of God has become the Shepherd of His people, and He so shepherds them that they neither hunger nor thirst, neither does the sun make them weary nor the hardness of the way distress them, for He leads them by still waters and living fountains, and with the gentleness of a mother God wipes away every tear from their eyes. I believe in holiness because I believe in the Great Shepherd.

God has put it in the covenant. Through the blood of the everlasting covenant the prayer for perfection is made. God has sworn by an oath. Every word of God is sure, but of this word He has given surety. It is His will we should be made perfect in every good thing to do His will. His only begotten Son is surety for His Word. He has undertaken it on covenant terms. It is a wonderful covenant, for in it God pledges Himself and undertakes for us. I love the covenant relationship. The blood of the cross is the security for our perfecting. I believe in Holiness because I believe in the covenant through the blood of the cross. Even that is not all. He works in us that which He wills to do for us. He works in us to will His will and to do His good pleasure. The end of it all is that we so live as to be well-pleasing in His sight. That is the Christian Perfection set forth in the great prayer which closes the Epistle on the Perfect Son, the Perfect Saviour, and the Perfect Salvation. How can I but believe that such a Saviour is able to save to the uttermost, and make me perfect in every good thing to do His Will?

Jesus, the First and Last,
On Thee my soul is cast:

The Prayer for Christian Perfection

Thou didst Thy work begin
By blotting out my sin;
Thou wilt the root remove,
And perfect me in love.

Yet when the work is done,
The work is but begun:
Partaker of Thy grace,
I long to see Thy face;
The first I prove below,
The last I die to know.

The Call To Holiness

There is no doubt about the call. It is on every page of the Scriptures, and the reason for it is in the nature and character of God. Holiness is not optional, but imperative. Because God is holy, His people must be holy. Without holiness no man can see the Lord. It is imperative. It must be possible. He who wills the end must provide the means. The will of God is our sanctification. The command of God is that we be holy. If sanctification is His will, and holiness His command, He must have made it possible; otherwise He would mock us and call us to an unequal and unfair task. Life would be doomed to disappointment and dissatisfaction, failure and condemnation.

When God calls us to holiness it is frankly admitted that the demand is beyond us. We cannot attain unto holiness. God gives what we cannot gain by will or effort of our own. Sanctification is not attained; it is obtained. For it is of grace through faith and not of merit by works. It is without price, because it is priceless, and it is not of works, because it is beyond man's possibility. He who wills our sanctification is Himself the Sanctifier.

❧ THE WILL OF GOD ❧

God wills our sanctification. Of that there is no doubt. It is not a doctrine of man to be accepted or declined. We are called unto holiness, and God requires His people to be holy because He is holy. His holiness is the pattern, and His people are to be holy because He is holy, and His holiness is the pattern and standard of His demand. Absolute holiness belongs to God alone, and when He commands that His people be holy as He is holy, it means that every quality of holiness in Him must be in them, even as Jesus commanded, "Be ye therefore perfect, even as your Father which is in heaven is perfect."[1] What He wills He commands. "For God hath not called us unto uncleanness, but unto holiness. He therefore that despiseth, despiseth not man, but God, who hath also given unto us his holy Spirit".[2] To reject the call is to reject God -- to despise God. To deny the call is to deny the Holy Spirit.

The will of God is our sanctification. Will implies purpose, purpose is dependent upon power, and power assumes provision. What God wills to be He must be able to do; what He requires He must make possible. Will implies freedom, our freedom as well as His. God cannot make saints as He makes worlds. When He wills man's sanctification, another will is involved. Man cannot be sanctified even by God apart from consent and without cooperation. The thirty-sixth chapter of Ezekiel is the chapter of God's "I wills." At the end

---

[1] Matthew 5:48
[2] 1 Thessalonians 4:7,8

of the chapter God says: " I the LORD have spoken *it*, and I will do *it*,"[3] and immediately adds another "I will": " Thus saith the Lord GOD; I will yet *for* this be enquired of by the house of Israel, to do *it* for them."[4] God's will waits for man's will; and God's power is conditioned upon man's consent. His will is plainly our sanctification.

✌ THE ACT OF GOD ✣

Saints are God's workmanship. Sanctification is the act of God. Concerning this, the Word of God is decisive and emphatic. Saint Paul prays in the Thessalonian epistle -- " And the very God of peace sanctify you wholly."[5] It is the Lord who separates the godly unto Himself, and He alone can make that which is separated to be holy in nature and character. There is a cleansing required that is beyond man's power, and there is a sanctification to be wrought that God alone can do. The carnal mind is rooted in the subsoil of human nature, and man knows that he cannot make himself clean. Sanctification is not by the will of man. Neither prayer nor discipline, Bible study nor fasting, penance nor ordinance, can purify the heart and sanctify the nature. It takes God to do that. He is able. He Himself does that which He wills and commands.

The experience of sanctification is variously ascribed to God, to Christ, and to the Holy Spirit. We are sanctified through Christ; our Lord sanctified Himself that we might be

---

[3] Ezekiel 36:36
[4] V. 37
[5] 1 Thessalonians 5:23

sanctified, and we are sanctified through the offering of the body of Christ once for all (Heb. 10:10). We are sanctified with the blood of Christ (Heb. 13:12) and the blood of Jesus Christ his Son cleanseth us from all sin, (I John 1:7). We are sanctified through the Word of God. "The word is truth," (John 15:3-17; I John 1:7). We are made holy through the sanctification of the Holy Spirit (Rom. 15:16; 1 Cor. 6:11; II Thess. 2:13; I Peter 1:2). From first to the last, salvation is of grace through faith. As we are justified by faith, so are we sanctified by faith.

☜ THE WORK OF GOD ☞

There is a tense in the Greek that indicates an act and implies a process. The act is definite and complete, and it establishes a subsequent and consequent order. That is the tense of the sanctifying act of God. It is a definite experience,

> *It is a tragedy when "holiness" people are not holy people.*

specific in character, and verified by the assurance of the Spirit. It is a second work of grace involving a crisis, making an end and establishing a beginning. The act initiates a new order, a new stage of development, and a new inheritance of maturity. The son comes of age. The experience equips and endows. No state of grace is static, no growth in grace is final, no work of grace is unrelated.

We do not grow *into* the experience of sanctification, but we grow *in* it; there is no perfection beyond which there is no perfecting. The holy have their fruit unto holiness. The branch in the vine is cleansed, that it may bring forth more fruit; the call to holiness is a call to a holy life. It is a tragedy when "holiness" people are not holy people.

The act of God in sanctification is followed by the work of God in holiness of character and life. "And the Lord make you to increase and abound in love one toward another, and toward all *men*, even as we *do* toward you: To the end he may stablish your hearts unblameable in holiness before God, even our Father, at the coming of our Lord Jesus Christ with all his saints." (I Thess. 3:12,13).

❧ WHEN DOES GOD SANCTIFY? ☙

If a man must be holy to see God, there must be some point at which the work is done. Because the blessing seems impossible outside heaven, there are many who believe that it takes place at death. There is no Scripture authority for such belief, and death is never said to be either the time or the means of sanctification. Many regard holiness as a state toward which we continually strive but never attain. It is thus always an ideal and never an experience, but God speaks of it as an act, and treats it as an experience. The Scriptures never identify it with the new birth. They urge it upon the regenerate as an inheritance, and command it as an obligation. John Fletcher of Madeley has answered the question of time:

"If our hearts are purified by faith, as the Scriptures expressly testify, if the faith which peculiarly purifies the heart of Christians is a faith in the promise of the Father, which promise was made by the Son, and directly points at a peculiar effusion of the Holy Spirit, the purifier of spirits; if we may believe in a moment, and if God may in a moment seal our sanctifying faith by sending us a fullness of His sanctifying Spirit; if this, I say, is the case, does it not follow, that to deny the possibility of the instantaneous destruction of sin, is to deny that we can make an instantaneous act of faith in the sanctifying promise of the Father, and in the all-cleansing blood of the Son, and that God can seal that act by an instantaneous operation of His Spirit?"[6]

Nothing surprised nor distressed John Wesley so much as the number of those who entered into the blessing of entire sanctification and lost it. The same disastrous experience is with us. The moral failures are largely responsible for the unbelief that despises the blessing. The strain of trying to live the holy life is intolerable if the life itself declines. It is only possible with God, and the conditions of life and growth are constant and uncompromising.

If the experience is not to end in disappointment and dishonor, there must be the work of God that establishes in holiness. The garden of God can suffer no neglect. Holiness involves diligence in cultivation, watchfulness in discipline, attention to nourishment, and exercise in Godlikeness. The perfect must go on unto perfection, and the sanctified must perfect holiness in the fear of the Lord. The God that sanctifies can keep, and His keeping is as complete as His sanctifying.

---

[6] Wallace, J.L. (Ed.)., Fletcher, J., The Works of John Fletcher, Volume 3: Doctrines of Grace and Justice, Brookfield, Missouri: Apprehending Truth Publishers.

He keeps the spirit holy. He keeps the soul unspotted. He keeps the body sanctified, as becomes the temple of the indwelling God.

This whole subject is hopeless until it is approached from the Godward side. Man cannot make himself holy. He cannot keep himself holy. God can sanctify. God can keep. "Faithful is he that calleth you. who also will do it."[7]

> "Jesus, the First and Last,
> On Thee my soul is cast;
> Thou didst Thy work begin
> By blotting out my sin;
>
> Thou wilt the root remove,
> And perfect me in love.
> "Yet when the work is done
> The work is but begun;
>
> Partaker of Thy grace,
> I long to see Thy face;
> The first I prove below;
> The last I die to know."

❧ END ❧

Study Guide

Chapter I:
❧ The Accent of Wesley's Teaching ❧

1.   To what can Wesley's doctrine of conversion, assurance, and full salvation be traced?

2.   What was the first distinctive note of Wesley's creed?

3.   What is typically lost in a zeal for liberty?

4.   In plainest terms, what does Calvinism mean?

5.   Wesley's preaching and testimony struck down what doctrine?

6.   What harm is found in uncertainty? 6

7.   What follows the entire sanctification of believers?

8.   What was the core of the Gospel Wesley preached?

9.   Describe the archetype of a Christian nation's life.

Chapter II:
‹ꜣ The Doctrine of Christian Perfection ꜱ›

1. What changes content and loses value?

2. What is it that keeps many from seeking the true?

3. What are some ignorant questions asked by "clever" people?

4. What is the whole of Christian perfection according to John Wesley?

5. Testimony is impossible without _____.

Chapter III:
‹ꜣ What Christian Perfection Implies ꜱ›

1. Where is much of the difficulty in the subject of Christian Perfection?

2. What 3 angles of interpretation must be considered to complete our understanding of perfection?

3. What is meant by perfection?

4. What three things are absent from a life of perfection?

5. What is implied in redemption?

6. What happens to mans nature in spiritual death?

7. What are the essential elements in man's loss through sin?

Chapter IV:
✒ The Essential Element in Christian Perfection ✒

1. What is the essential principle of all moral evil?

2. In what does entire sanctification consist?

3. What do the 2 Covenants declare? Explain.

4. What is inherent in the divine character of God?

5. Why is it difficult to identify another man's perfect love simply from natural observation?

6. What is the only authorized test of love?

7. How is love made perfect?

Chapter V:
✒ Christian Perfection As Interpreted by John Wesley ✒

1. To what are the completeness and consistency of Wesley's doctrine and discipline attributed?

2. How do Calvinists view Christian Perfection?

3. What very nearly makes the cross the minister of sin?

4. What empowers obedience?

Chapter VI:
❧ Christian Perfection in Relation to Sins and Mistakes ❧

1. List 4 things concerning sin that the Apostle John's teachings settle for all time.

2. A child is born innocent and is protected under the covenant of sonship until when?

3. What settles sonship under spiritual parentage?

4. If sin is not the violation of a commandment or an act, what is it?

5. What is God's saving power conditioned upon?

6. What is a mistake?

7. What is the vision of the pure heart always discovering?

Chapter VII:
❧ Christian Perfection and Temptation ❧

1. What does it mean that Christ was tempted like as we are?

2. What does Grace destroy?

3. When man is sanctified, what become allies of his conscience?

4. When is desire sinful?

5. How does Satan seek to win us back?

6. What is the final temptation of spirit filled people?

Chapter VIII:
❧ Christian Perfection: A Second Blessing ❧

1. What is the cause of shrinking from the experience of the crisis of sanctification?

2. What are some more general terms used for entire sanctification and what is implied in their use?

3. What was the reproach of the Christians at Corinth?

4. What is comprehended in the "first" blessing?

5. What is brought by the "second" blessing?

6. What was the culmination of Charles Inwood's experience of sanctification?

Chapter IX:
❧ Do the Scriptures Teach a Second Blessing? ❧

1. By what proof does a man believe a doctrine?

2. How are Spiritual things discerned?

3. In what must experience be rooted and grounded?

4. What is more offensive than sins acts of transgression?

5. What is impossible without conviction?

Chapter X:
✑ Is Christian Perfection Attainable? ✑

1. What is not implied in Christian perfection?

2. What term did Wesley use for Christian perfection that is both Scriptural and intelligible?

3. What word implies 'possibility' in 1 John 2:6?

4. According to John Wesley's letter to Jenny Cooper, what 3 things are not present in Entire Sanctification?

5. Of what is this experience an mingling?

Chapter XI:
✑ The Negations of Christian Perfection ✑

1. What is one of the most common criticisms of holiness? Explain.

2. The absence of what will reveal the presence of glory?

3. What does 'no fear' mean?

4. What is perfect peace?

5. When is "Ataraxia" possible?

6. Name 3 negations of Christian Perfection.

Study Guide

Chapter XII:
❧ Difficulties About Christian Perfection ❧

1. What is the mischief in agreeing that holiness comes by a gradual growth in grace?

2. What is inconsistent with "gradual growth in grace"? Why?

3. What does the author consider is "rather confused logic"?

4. What brings the soul into fellowship with Christ?

5. Where is the real difficulty in perfection?

6. What Biblical text is the best statement of the doctrine and expression of perfection?

Chapter XIII:
❧ The Prayer for Christian Perfection ❧

1. Why is it best for a man not to profess his own perfection?

2. Where should the witness to our perfection be found?

3. What are two things concerning perfection that we should pray for?

4. What things are necessary to do God's will?

5. What is Christian Perfection as it relates to Gods will?

6. What is the security for our perfecting?

⚘ The Call to Holiness ⚘

1. How do we know that holiness is possible?

2. What is the pattern and standard of God's demand that His people be holy?

3. What 2 things must exist between God and man for his sanctification?

4. To whom is the experience of sanctification ascribed?

5. What follows the act of God in sanctification?

6. For some, holiness is always an ideal but never an _____. Why?

7. What does holiness involve?

For answers to Study Guide questions and more interactive content please visit:

http://www.publishers.apprehendingtruth.net/chadwick.html

Apprehending Truth Publishers

Proclaiming Truth in the Age of Deceit

AD LEGEM MAGIS ET AD TESTIMONIUM

For additional copies of this book and a list of other titles
available from Apprehending Truth please visit our website:

http://www.publishers.apprehendingtruth.net

30550122R00068

Printed in Great Britain
by Amazon